1 MONTH OF FREE READING

at

www.ForgottenBooks.com

By purchasing this book you are eligible for one month membership to ForgottenBooks.com, giving you unlimited access to our entire collection of over 1,000,000 titles via our web site and mobile apps.

To claim your free month visit:
www.forgottenbooks.com/free892913

* Offer is valid for 45 days from date of purchase. Terms and conditions apply.

ISBN 978-0-266-81018-6
PIBN 10892913

This book is a reproduction of an important historical work. Forgotten Books uses state-of-the-art technology to digitally reconstruct the work, preserving the original format whilst repairing imperfections present in the aged copy. In rare cases, an imperfection in the original, such as a blemish or missing page, may be replicated in our edition. We do, however, repair the vast majority of imperfections successfully; any imperfections that remain are intentionally left to preserve the state of such historical works.

Forgotten Books is a registered trademark of FB &c Ltd.
Copyright © 2018 FB &c Ltd.
FB &c Ltd, Dalton House, 60 Windsor Avenue, London, SW19 2RR.
Company number 08720141. Registered in England and Wales.

For support please visit www.forgottenbooks.com

Historic, archived document

Do not assume content reflects current scientific knowledge, policies, or practices.

P. J. BERCKMANS CO.
INCORPORATED.

FRUITLAND NURSERIES

Established 1856

AUGUSTA, GEORGIA

1915-1916

L. A. BERCKMANS, Pres.
R. C. BERCKMANS, Vice-Pres.
P. J. A. BERCKMANS, Jr., Sec. and Treas.

INDEX

	Page
Abelia	37, 51
Acacia	22, 31
Acer	31, 32
Adam's Needle	48
Aesculus	32
Akebia	48
Aleurites	32
Allamanda	48
Almonds	17
Althaea	22
Ampelopsis	48-49
Antigonon	49
Apple, Flowering Crab	34
Apples	9, 10
Apple, Crab	10
Apricots	11
Arborvitaes	54, 55, 60, 61
Arbutus	37
Ardisia	37
Arundo	53
Asclepias	30
Ashberry, Holly-leaved	45
Aucuba	37, 38
Azalea	23, 38
Bamboosa aurea	53
Barberry	23, 38, 51
Bay Tree	43
Bear Grass	48
Berberis	23, 38, 45, 51
Bignonia	49
Bilsted	33
Biota	54, 55, 60
Blackberry	19
Bottle Brush	45
Boxwood	38, 39, 52
Buddleia	23
Butterfly Weed	30
Buxus	38, 39, 52
Calico Bush	43
Callicarpa	23
Callistemon	45
Calycanthus	23
Camellia	39
Camphor Tree	40
Candle Nut	32
Caryopteris	23
Cassia	23
Catalpa	32
Ceanothus	23
Cedar	55
Cedrus	55
Celtis	32
Cephalotaxus	55
Cerasus	32, 40, 52
Cercis	23, 24, 32
Chamaerops	40
Chamaecyparis	59, 60
Cherry, Carolina	40
Cherry, Flowering	32
Chestnut	17
Chilopsis	24
Chionanthus	24
Chrysanthemums	30
Cinnamomum	40
Citrange	20, 40
Citrus trifoliata	24, 52
Citrus Fruits	40, 41
Cladrastis	36
Clematis	49
Cleyera	41
Climbers and Trailers	48, 49, 50, 51
Conifers, specimen	60, 61
Corchorus	24
Cornus	24, 33
Cotoneaster	41
Crataegus	41

	Page
Cunninghamia	55
Cupressus	55, 56, 59, 60
Cydonia	24
Cypress	55, 56, 59, 60
Deutzia	24
Dewberry	19
Diervilla	30
Diospyros	15, 16
Diseases, Fungus	5, 6, 7
Dogwood	24, 33
Elaeagnus	21, 41, 42
Elm	36
English Laurel	43
Eriobotrya	21, 42
Escallonia	42
Eulalia	53
Euonymus	49
Exochorda	25
Ficus	50
Figs	11
Filberts	17
Fire Bush	24
Forsythia	25
Fringe	24
Fungicides and Insecticides	7
Gardenia	42
Gelsemium	50
Ginkgo	35
Golden Bell	25
Grape Fruit	41
Grapes	19, 20
Grasses, Ornamental	53
Gynerium	53
Hackberry	32
Hedera	50
Hedge Plants	51, 52
Hibiscus	22, 25, 30
Holly	42, 43
Honeysuckle	26, 27, 50
Horse Chestnuts	32
Hydrangea	25, 26
Hypericum	26
Ilex	42, 43
Illicium	43
Insects, Injurious	5, 6
Iris	30
Ivy	50
Jasmine	26, 50
Jasminum	26, 50
Judas Tree	23
Juniper	57, 58, 60
Juniperus	57, 58, 60
Kadsura	50
Kalmia	43
Kerria	24, 27
Kinkan	41
Koelreutaria	33
Kumquat	41
Lagerstroemia	26
Laurel	43
Laurocerasus	43
Laurus	43
Laurustinus	47
Lawn Grass Seed	8
Lemons	41
Libocedrus	58
Ligustrum	43, 44, 52
Lilac	29
Linden	36
Liquidambar	33

	Page
Liriodendron	33
Locust	28
Lonicera	26, 27, 50
Loquat	42
Magnolia	33, 34, 44, 45
Mahonia	45
Maidenhair Tree	35
Mallow	30
Malus	34
Maple	81, 32
Medlar, Japan	21, 42
Melia	34
Metrosideros	45
Mimosa	31
Mock Orange	27
Morus	34
Mulberries	21
Mulberry, French	23
Mulberry, Weeping	34
Myrtle	45
Myrtle, Crape	26
Myrtle, Trailing	51
Myrtus	45
Nandina, Japanese	45
Nectarines	11
Nerium	15
Nettle Tre	32
Nut Trees	17, 18
Oak	35, 46
Olea Fragrans	46
Oleander	45
Oleaster, Japan	21, 24, 25
Olive	21
Olive, Tea or Sweet	46
Oranges	20, 41
Orange. Hardy	24, 52
Osier Dogwood	24
Osmanthus	46
Oxydendron	34
Palm, Chusan Fan	40
Pampas Grass	53
Parasol, Japan	36
Parthenocissus	50
Peach, Flowering	34, 35
Peaches	11, 12, 13, 14
Pearl Bush	25
Pears	14, 15
Pecans	18
Peonies	30
Periwinkle	51
Persica	34
Persimmon, Japanese	15, 16
Philadelphus	27
Phoenix	46
Photinia	46
Phyllistachys	53
Pine	58, 59
Pine, Chinese	55
Pinus	58, 59
Pittosporum	46
Plane Tree	35
Platanus	35
Plum, Purple Leaf	35
Plums	16, 17, 27
Podocarpus	55
Pomegranate	21, 27
Popinac	22
Poplar	35
Populus	35
Potato Vine	51
Poupartia	35
Privet	43, 44, 52
Prunus	27, 35
Pumps, Spray	8
Punica	27
Pyramidal Boxwood	39
Pyrus	24

	Page
Quercus	35, 46
Quince, Japan	24
Quinces	17
Raphiolepsis Indica	47
Raspberries	19
Red Bud	32
Retinospora	59, 60, 61
Reed, Giant	53
Rhododendron	47
Rhodotypus	27
Rhus	27
Rhynchospermum	50
Robinia	28
Rosemary	28
Rose, Mexican	49
Rose of Sharon	22
Roses	61, 62, 63, 64
Rosemarinus	28
Salisburia	35
Salix	35
Salvia Greggi	28
Smoke Tree	27
Snowball	30
Snowberry	29
Solanum	51
Sourwood	34
Spanish Bayonet	48
Spiraea	28, 52
Spiraea, Blue	23
Spondias	35
Spray Pumps	8
Stephanandra	28
Sterculia	36
St. John's Wort, Golden	26
Storax	28
Strawberry Shrub	23
Strawberry Tree	37
Styrax	28
Sugarberry	32
Sulpho-Tobacco Soap	7
Sumac	27
Sweet Gum	33
Sweet Shrub	23
Sycamore	35
Symphoricarpos	29
Syringa	27, 29
Tamarisk	29
Tamarix	29
Taxodium	36
Tea, New Jersey	23
Tea, Olive	46
Tea Plant, Chinese	47
Thea	47
Thuya	60, 61
Tilia	36
Tulip Tree	33
Trumpet Vine	49
Ulmus	36
Umbrella Tree, Texas	34
Varnish Tree	36
Viburnum	30, 47, 52
Vinca	51
Virgilia	36
Virginia Creeper	48, 49
Vitex	30
Walnuts	17
Weigela	30
Willow	35
Wistaria	51
Yellow Wood	36
Yew, False	55
Yucca	48

The A. J. Showalter Co., Printers and Binders, Dalton, Ga.

P. J. Berckmans Co., Inc.
Landscape Architects
1012 Chronicle Building   Phone 992
Augusta, Georgia

THE services of the Landscape Architect, in the arrangement of land for utilitarian and aesthetic purposes, are now considered, by people of advanced ideas, fully as valuable as are those of the Building Architect in his field. With the maturity of well planned landscape work throughout the country, has come a growing appreciation of artistic design, and a realization that good results, in work of this character, can best be obtained through the assistance of a well-trained Landscape Architect.

The work of the Landscape Architect may be defined as: "The arrangement of land, and of the features on that land, for the purpose of utility and beauty." This definition at once contradicts the prevailing idea that the work of the Profession is aesthetic solely—that it is the mere embellishment of land after all practical development has been completed. In reality, in landscape designing, problems concerning utility are always the first to be studied; decoration or embellishment being the second consideration. If possible, the Landscape Architect and Building Architect should begin their work simultaneously and continue to co-operate in the development of plans, so that all designs for buildings and grounds may be harmonious.

The P. J. Berckmans Company, Inc., respectfully offers its services, as Landscape Architects, to all persons who are interested in the laying out of land for practical and aesthetic purposes. The men who have charge of this work have had the best of technical training in the Schools of Landscape Architecture in Harvard University and in the State College of Pennsylvania; and have traveled extensively in this country and abroad for the purpose of studying the best work in landscape design. Their knowledge of the flora, suitable for landscape work in this section of the country, is the result of the firm's fifty years of experience.

The practice of this office includes the making of reports, designs and specifications for the development of large country estates, the grounds of suburban or city homes (the small place often needs the more careful attention), formal and informal gardens, garden accessories, such as, pergolas, fountains and garden houses; the grounds of country clubs, golf clubs, educational institutions and public buildings; parks and park-ways, cemeteries, playgrounds, industrial villages and land sub-divisions. It is prepared, also, to give advice upon forest culture and problems in city planning.

Professional Methods—A visit to the property, and a consultation with the owner, is the first step. If buildings are to be erected, the Landscape Architect, Building Architect and owner should consult to determine the best location and to outline the general arrangement of important features. This frequently saves expense and enables the Landscape Architect to work out the best design. If a topographical survey has not been made, this is the next step. Over this plat, a preliminary plan is then prepared and submitted to the client. When this has been approved, working drawings are prepared. If desired, the Landscape Architect will furnish a superintendent to carry out the plans.

Planting Plans—Planting is studied as a part of the complete design, in the arrangement of plantings, the object is to secure harmonious groupings according to general growth, texture and color. The adaptability of plants to soil and climatic conditions is carefully considered.

Charge—Charges are made on a per diem basis, for time used in traveling and in the preparation of reports, plans and specifications. All traveling and living expenses are rendered as additional charge. When several clients are visited on one trip, traveling expenses are proportioned among them.

A folder, giving more detailed information, will be furnished on request.

P. J. BERCKMANS CO.

Suggestions

Always address all communications to P. J. BERCKMANS COMPANY, Drawer 1070, Augusta, Ga., and not to individuals.

NOTE All quotations are for immediate acceptance, subject to stock being sold. No liability to attach to us where frost, drought or other casualties beyond our control prevent delivery of stock that may be contracted for.

ORDER NOW—Do not wait until you are ready to plant. Frequently orders sent late in the season cannot be filled in full. Send us your order now; it will be carefully filed until you desire it shipped. When making out your order, write the full and correct name of the article desired, as given in catalogue. Give size and catalogue price. Never give local names of plants, as different plants frequently have the same local names.

RESERVING ORDERS—When purchasers desire these to be reserved for weeks or months after the opening of the shipping season, they must be paid for in full at the time of ordering.

NAME AND ADDRESS—Always write your name plainly upon order-sheet in catalogue. A lady should always sign herself Miss or Mrs., and always use the same initials.

Give your postoffice, county and state, also street or postoffice box number, and the name of your nearest express office.

SHIPPING DIRECTIONS—Give plain and explicit directions for shipping. If by freight, state route. When no directions are given, we shall use our best judgment in forwarding; but in all cases shipments are at purchaser's risk after receipt is taken from the transportation company. Freight and express rates will be given upon application.

EXPRESS—In all cases, when possible, we advise our customers to have their goods forwarded by express. Plants, trees, etc., are taken at a special reduced rate.

PARCEL POST—Owing to the nature of our products, we can send very few plants by Parcel Post, but if order can be sent this way, sufficient amount to cover postage must accompany order; otherwise it will be sent by express.

PACKING is free, except on export orders. These require large quantities of specially prepared packing material, and entail much extra labor and care in preparation. On such orders we charge the extra packing at actual cost. We maintain a large force of expert packers and only the most experienced men are entrusted with the packing.

TERMS OF PAYMENT—Cash with order, or satisfactory reference before, shipment; or, if preferred, will ship goods with Bill of Lading attached to Sight Draft, through express or bank. On all C. O. D. and Sight Draft orders we require 25 per cent. of the bill remitted before shipment.

PRICES—All prices quoted are net. We offer no premiums, discounts, or gratuities. Five trees or plants of a class will be billed at the 10 rate; 40 trees at the 100 rate; 400 at the 1,000 rate, viz; Five Pecans will be billed at the 10 rate; 40 at the 100 rate, etc.

REMITTANCES—Remittances should be made by Postoffice of Express Money Orders, or by checks on Augusta or New York. As our banks charge exchange on checks on all points except Augusta and New York please add fourth of 1 per cent on private checks. We cannot be held responsible for losses when remittances are not made as directed above. Cash sent through the mails is at sender's risk. Make all remittances payable to P. J. Berckmans Company.

WE GUARANTEE every tree or plant to be in a perfectly healthy condition, up to grade and first-class in every respect when leaving our hands, but, after delivering to forwarders, all losses resulting from delays or exposures in transit are at risk of purchaser.

RESPONSIBILITY—We have no connection whatever with any other nursery, and our responsibility extends only to persons purchasing direct from us. We are not responsible for failures arising from defective planting, unfavorable weather conditions, for improper treatment and cultivation. While we exercise the greatest care to have all of our trees and plants true to name, well grown, and packed in the best possible manner, and hold ourselves in readiness to replace all trees and plants that may accidentally prove untrue to label, free of charge, or refund the amount paid, therefore, it is mutually understood and agreed between the purchaser and ourselves that our guarantee of genuineness shall not in any case make us liable for any sum greater than that originally received for such trees or plants as prove untrue.

ERRORS—We exercise the utmost care in filling orders, and always put in more than is ordered, but during the rush of the busy season an error is occasionally made, and satisfactory correction will be promptly made upon notification. Keep a copy of your order for comparison. All claims for errors must be made within five days after receipt of goods; otherwise they will not be entertained.

SHIPPING FACILITIES—Augusta being the terminal point of seven lines of railroads, and two lines of steamers upon the Savannah River, enables us to secure low rates of freight to all points.

SHIPPING SEASON—This usually commences about the middle of October, or as soon as the plants are sufficiently dormant to lift with safety, and for all open ground trees and plants continues until the middle of March, or until the buds begin to swell. Pot-grown plants can be safely sent out any time of the year.

INSECTS AND DISEASES—Our Nurseries are free from disease. Certificate of State Entomologist is attached to every shipment.

FUMIGATION—We fumigate our stock with hydrocyanic acid gas before shipping, as required by state law, so that assurance of freedom from insects or diseases of any kind is made doubly sure.

Number of Trees or Plants on an Acre at Given Distances Apart

Distance apart each way.	Number of plants.	Distance apart each way.	Number of plants.	Distance apart each way.	Number of plants.
1 foot	43,560	8 feet	680	18 feet	134
2 feet	10,890	9 feet	537	20 feet	108
3 feet	4,840	10 feet	435	25 feet	70
4 feet	2,722	12 feet	302	30 feet	48
5 feet	1,742	13 feet	258	35 feet	35
6 feet	1,210	15 feet	193	40 feet	27
7 feet	888	16 feet	170	50 feet	17

AUGUSTA, GEORGIA.

Hints for Planters

Time for Planting—In this climate, vegetation, although inactive in winter for the formation of leaves and new wood, is never so as to new roots. A tree transplanted in the early winter will, by the ensuing spring, have grown sufficient new roots to give it a firm hold in the ground, and will grow off rapidly when active vegetation commences. Plant as early after the first killing frost as practicable, although hardy stock can be safely transplanted any time during the winter when the ground is not wet or frozen. Planting can be continued until the middle of March, or until just before the buds begin to swell.

Preparation of the Soil—The most desirable soil for fruit trees is a rich loam, naturally dry or made so by drainage. Peaches and plums must be planted on high, well-drained soil. Before planting, prepare the land by thoroughly plowing and subsoiling, first using a two-horse plow, followed by a subsoil plow. Lay off the rows at required distances, and dig holes at least two feet wide and two feet deep; fill the holes by breaking in the sides, commencing at the bottom and going upward. Use surface soil in filling up, and with this mix one or two shovelfuls of thoroughly decomposed barnyard manure, or use one or two pounds of good bone meal. All fertilizers must be thoroughly incorporated with the soil. Avoid the contact of the roots with heating manures.

We strongly advocate digging holes with dynamite whenever feasible.

Preparation of Trees and How to Plant—Before planting, remove the broken roots; cut back one-year peach, apple, pear, cherry and plum trees to a naked stem 1½ to 2½ feet high, leaving no side branches. Two-year-old trees should have their branches cut back to half their length or less; the lower limbs less than those above, cutting in shorter as you go upward, leaving the leader the longest. (For pruning peach trees, see page 11). The tree should be set about 2 inches deeper than it stood in the nursery.

Cultivation—You cannot expect to get good results from your trees unless you keep them well cultivated. The soil must be frequently stirred during summer. The area immediately around the trees must be kept free from grass and weeds, and this portion of the orchard should receive especial attention. All suckers or branches which start below the head of the tree should be removed. For the first two years cultivate the orchard during summer in some crop suited to the location, such as cotton, vegetables, melons, peas, peanuts, velvet or soy beans, giving the preference to leguminous crops. Never plant corn or small grain in your orchard.

It is always advisable to sow in the fall a cover crop, such as clover, vetch or rye, using a suitable fertilizer. Turn under this cover crop in early spring. When soils are deficient in lime and potash, supply this deficiency with an application of lime, bone meal, hardwood ashes or high grade commercial fertilizer, as the soil requires. Satisfactory results cannot be expected unless the orchard is supplied with the proper plant food and receives careful cultivation.

Selection of Trees—For this climate, experience has taught us that one and two-year-old trees of thrifty growth (except peaches, only one-year trees of which should be planted) are the most desirable. Purchasers should bear in mind that such trees can be removed from the nursery with all their roots, whereas a four or five-year-old tree cannot be taken up without cutting away a large portion of them. Success in transplanting is increased according as attention is paid in selecting well-rooted trees, instead of heavily-branched ones. Give as many sound roots and as little head to a tree as possible.

Care of the Trees on Arrival—If not ready to plant on arrival, unpack without exposing the roots to cold or air; dig a trench, and heel-in by carefully covering the roots with earth, and give a copious watering. Trees thus treated can remain in the trenches until ready for planting in the orchard. If frozen when received, do not open the boxes, but place them in a cellar or some cool, dark room that is free from frost, and let them remain until all frost is drawn out. If no cellar or frost-proof room, bury the box in sawdust or dirt until thawed. The point is to get the frost entirely out without sudden exposure of stock to heat, light or air. Even if frozen solid, the stock will not be injured if handled in this manner.

Injurious Insects and Fungus Diseases

We only enumerate the most abundant and destructive insects and fungus diseases which infest our orchards and gardens. The remedies as suggested are in accordance with the latest recommendations of the leading Entomologists.

Previous to spraying during the dormant season all trees and plants should be properly pruned. The proper time for applying spray solutions cannot be given exactly in this calendar. Allowances for difference in climatic and weather conditions between different localities must be considered. The orchardist should familiarize himself with the habits and life history of the different insects and diseases, in order that he may apply to his particular locality and conditions the necessary measures.

APPLES.

Apple Worm (Coddling Moth)—Spray with two pounds of Standard Arsenate of Lead, three pounds of lime to each fifty gallons of water; first when the buds open, just before blooming; second, so soon as the petals fall and before the calyx closes; third, three weeks later; fourth, about ten weeks after the petals fall.

When the time comes for using the third spraying, Bordeaux Mixture should be combined with one and one-half pounds of Arsenate of Lead. The Bordeaux Mixture is used at this time to prevent Bitter Rot and other fungus diseases.

Apple Tree Blight—Same treatment as recommended for Pear Blight.

Bitter Rot—Use Lime-Sulphur Solution one and one-fourth gallons, two pounds of Arsenate of Lead to each fifty gallons of water. Spray as soon as petals fall. Give a second application of this same mixture three or four weeks after petals fall; then about eight weeks after petals fall use Bordeaux Mixture, (4-4-50) with the addition of two pounds Arsenate of Lead, and repeat this latter spraying every two weeks until four applications of same have been given.

Borer—Keep orchard free from litter and examine trees regularly for borers. Their presence will be indicated by sawdust at the entance of their burrows. Remove, if near the surface, by means of a knife or wire. For those that have entered to a considerable depth inject, by means of a medicine dropper, a small quantity of carbon bi-sulphide in their excavation and seal securely with putty or wax.

Canker Worm—Encircle the tree with a canvas belt thoroughly coated with tar; also spray with arsenate of lead as soon as worms appear; two pounds of arsenate of lead, three pounds of lime to fifty gallons of water. If necessary repeat in three or four days.

Caterpillar—Destroy nests as soon as they appear in the spring by burning, or spraying with two pounds of arsenate of lead, three pounds of lime to fifty gallons of water.

Cedar Rust—Use seven pounds of atomic sulphur, two pounds of arsenate of lead to each fifty gallons of water. Spray the trees at the same period as recommended for Scab.

Green or Black Aphis—Spray with Black Leaf 40 at the rate of one part to two or three parts of water, as soon as the Aphis appear.

San Jose Scale—For dormant spraying, use Thomsen Chemical Company's lime-sulphur solution mixed at the rate of one gallon to eight gallons of water. Spray as early in the fall as trees are dormant, and again later in February and early March if the orchard is badly infested. For summer would suggest spraying with kerosene emulsion, one part of the emulsion to five parts of water.

5

P. J. BERCKMANS CO.

Scab—Use one and one-fourth gallons of lime sulphur solution, two pounds of arsenate of lead to each fifty gallons of water. Spray first, just before buds open; second, repeat as soon as petals fall; third, three or four weeks after petals fall; fourth, eight weeks after petals fall.

Woolly Aphis (Schizoneura lanigera) — for above-ground colonies, spray with Black Leaf 40, 1 part to 200 parts of water, or a tobacco decoction. The summer spray of 1½ gallons of lime-sulphur to 50 gallons of water will also kill them, but must be applied with great force.

For root-inhabiting colonies, remove the soil to a depth of about three inches, or sufficient to partially expose the roots; open a circle from four to eight feet in diameter, depending on the spread of the roots; distribute three to eight pounds of tobacco dust or use 10 per cent kerosene emulsion. Enough emulsion should be used to saturate the soil to a depth of three or four inches. Recent experiments have shown that kerosene emulsion may be used with success. Tobacco dust is of more value as a preventive and fertilizer. Badly infested trees should be treated with kerosene emulsion, applying this in April or May, but be sure to have the stock solution properly made or it may injure the trees.

BLACKBERRIES.

Rust—Use a spray of sulphate of copper solution; one part to fifteen gallons of water before buds break. Use Bordeaux Mixture (4-6-50) if Rust appears in spring or summer.

GRAPES.

Black Rot—Use Bordeaux mixture (3-4-50). Spray first, when leaves have expanded; second, just after fruit has set; repeat every two weeks until fruit is nearly grown.

Borer (Prionus)—Its presence is manifested by the unhealthy appearance of the vine. Search must be made at the roots and the grub destroyed.

Curculio—Use Bordeaux Mixture (3-4-50), adding two pounds of arsenate of lead. Spray, first, before blooming; second, when fruit is about one-eighth inch in diameter; third, about first or fifteenth of July.

Flea Beetle—Use two pounds of arsenate of lead, three pounds of lime to fifty gallons of water. Spray as buds are swelling and a second time about two weeks later.

Leaf Folder (Desmia funeralis)—Kerosene emulsion or paris green or arsenate of lead as a spray.

Mildew—This can be controlled by Bordeaux mixture same as recommended for Black Rot.

JAPAN PERSIMMONS, WALNUTS AND PECANS.

Borer (Prionus)—These bore through the roots and usually destroy the tree, and must be carefully removed. Carefully examine collar of tree in winter and mid-summer, and apply lime-sulphur wash.

Caterpillar (Catocala mæstosa)—Feeds on the leaves of pecans, and is sometimes quite injurious. Spray with paris green four ounces, lime one pound, to fifty gallons of water.

Pecan Bud Worm (Proteopteryx deludana)—Spray the trees just as the buds are opening, with arsenate of lead, three pounds to fifty gallons of water, and two pounds of lime, and repeat application ten days later. If the worms appear again in June or July, repeat the treatment. This will also help control the pecan husk borer.

Twig Girdlers (Oncideres cingulatus)—All limbs that have been girdled and have fallen must be burned at once, thus destroying all future broods of sawyers.

White Fly—One and one-half ounces of Schnarr's Insecticide to 100 gallons of water, or whale-oil soap 1 to 1½ ounces to 1 gallon of water, or Thomsen Chemical Company's lime-sulphur solution, 1 part to 25 parts of water.

PEACHES AND PLUMS.

Peach Tree Borer (Sanninoidea exitiosa)—The old method of worming peach trees in winter has been found ineffective, principally because the worms cause too much damage before being removed.

In the spring remove the earth from about the body of the tree down to the crown, scraping off gummy exudations, and carefully search for the borer. For this work use a farrier's knife or a tool especially made for worming peach trees.

An excellent wash for borers is the following: One bushel of quicklime, 20 pounds of sulphur, 1 gallon of coal-tar, 50 gallons of water. Mix tar and sulphur in 10 gallons of water and add lime. Stir well while slaking. When it is entirely slaked dilute the above to 50 gallons, and apply this wash to the tree, allowing it to run well down upon the roots. As soon as it is applied, draw up the earth to the tree so that it will form a cone about six inches above the level. A second application of this wash should be made during August. During the last of October remove the mound of earth from around the tree and thoroughly scrape the bark, as in the spring, and give another application of the wash. This is a vigorous treatment, but is effective in all cases.

Black Knot in Plums—Cut off the affected branches below affected parts and burn to prevent its spreading. Spray with bordeaux mixture.

Brown Rot on Peaches, Plums and Nectarines—As Brown Rot, Curculio and Scab work together, the same treatment is, therefore, recommended for all.

For Early and Mid-Season Varieties—First: Spray the trees about ten days after the petals fall, when the calyces or shucks are being pushed off, using 1½ pounds of tri-plumbic arsenate of lead and 3 pounds of lime to each 50 gallons of water. This is for the curculio and should be applied with a nozzle capable of throwing a fine spreading mist, covering the fruit and foliage with a very thin film of poison, but under no circumstances should the trees be drenched.

Second: About twenty days later, or one month after the petals fall, spray the trees with atomic sulphur, 5 pounds to 50 gallons of water, or self-boiled lime-sulphur (8-8-50). To this should be added 1½ pounds of tri-plumbic arsenate of lead, and where arsenate of lead is used, 3 pounds of lime to each 50 gallons of the spray. This is the second treatment for the curculio and the first treatment for scab and brown rot.

Third: About one month before the fruit is expected to ripen, spray the trees with atomic sulphur, 5 pounds to each 50 gallons of water, or with self-boiled lime-sulphur. No poison should be used at this time, and since the application is intended to prevent the development of brown rot during the month preceding the ripening of the fruit and during the picking season, the trees should be sprayed rather heavily so as to coat the fruit on all sides.

For Late Varieties—Late varieties should be sprayed with an additional application of atomic sulphur or self-boiled lime-sulphur about three weeks after the second treatment. This extra treatment is for the protection of the fruit from the attacks of peach scab, to which late maturing varieties are especially susceptible, as the interval between the second and third treatments would be much too long without it.

Curculio—To prevent the depredation of this pest see remedial measures under Brown Rot and Scab.

Peach and Plum Rosette—Root up and burn the affected tree as soon as the disease is observed.

San Jose Scale—Same treatment as recommended for Apples.

PEARS.

Pear Blight—Cut off and burn all affected limbs. Careful pruning should be resorted to during the winter to remove all affected limbs and affected areas. Disinfect the pruning shears after removing each branch or affected part. About a 4 per cent solution of formaldehyde can be used for this purpose.

Pear Blight is a bacterial disease and easily transmitted. Write to the State Board of Entomology, Atlanta, Ga., for bulletin on Pear Blight and Its Control; also to the Bureau of Plant Industry, Dept. of Agriculture, Washington, D. C.

San Jose Scale—Same treatment as recommended for Apples.

PECANS.

See under head of Japanese Persimmons, Walnuts and Pecans.

RASPBERRIES.

Rust—Same treatment as recommended for Blackberries.

ROSES.

Aphis—Spray plants with a solution of sulpho-tobacco soap; or a 2 per cent solution of lime-sulphur; or

AUGUSTA, GEORGIA.

tobacco water, using four ounces of tobacco-stems to one gallon of boiling water; strain the solution and add four ounces of soft soap while it is still hot; stir well to dissolve the soap.

Black Spot—This is a fungus disease. All diseased leaves should be removed from the plant, and those on the ground raked up and burned. Spray the plants with same strength of Bordeaux as recommended for mildew.

Leaf Hopper—Spray with insect powder, tobacco decoction or kerosene emulsion.

Mildew—This is caused by extremes of heat and cold, or by a continuance of damp, cold weather. Sprinkle the plants with water, and dust them with soot, or spray with Bordeaux mixture, 3-9-50, taking care to reach the under side of the leaves as well as the upper; also spray the ground around the plants.

Slugs—Spray with hellebore or insect powder.

Thrips and Other Insects—Same treatment as for Aphis.

SHADE TREES.

Leaf Eating Insects—Spray with two pounds of arsenate of lead, three pounds of lime to each fifty gallons of water.

San Jose Scale—Same treatment as recommended for Apples.

West India Scale—When trees are dormant use lime-sulphur solution as a spray, mixed with one gallon to eight of water. During the growing season use Schnarr's Insecticide, mixed 1½ gallons to 100 gallons of water.

WALNUTS.

See under head of Japanese Persimmons, Walnuts and Pecans.

Fungicide and Insecticide Solutions and Formulae

Arsenate of Lead can be used as a substitute for paris green and london purple. It can be used much stronger with less danger of injury to plants. Two pounds to fifty gallons of water will give good results against most biting insects. As a safeguard against injury to the foliage add three pounds of lime.

Atomic Sulphur (Thomsen's)—The best preventative against Brown Rot in Apples, Peaches, Plums and other fruits.

Bordeaux Mixture—Copper Sulphate, 4 pounds; quicklime, 6 pounds; water, 50 gallons. Dissolve the copper sulphate by putting it in a bag and hanging it in a wooden or earthen vessel holding 25 gallons; slake the lime gradually and add water until you have 25 gallons. The copper sulphate mixture and lime should then be poured into the pump so that the two streams will mix thoroughly as they fall. Bordeaux mixture will not keep more than twenty-four hours. Remember this.

Copper Sulphate Solution—Dissolve 1 pound of copper sulphate in 15 gallons of water. Do not apply this solution to foliage; it must be used before buds break on grape vines and peach trees. For the latter, use 25 gallons of water.

Kerosene Emulsion—One-half pound of soap dissolved in 1 gallon of water; add to this, while hot, 2 gallons of kerosene. (The boiling soap solution should be removed from the fire before the kerosene is added.) Churn violently with a spray pump or garden syringe until the mass becomes of the consistency of butter. Dilute the above mixture with from 9 to 15 parts of water when using, so that it will not be stronger than 1 part of oil to 9 to 15 parts of water. Sour milk may be used instead of soap.

Larkin's Sulpho-Tobacco Soap is a universal insecticide. A safe and sure exterminator of all kinds of insects and vermin on plants, shrubbery, vines, small fruits and trees. The soap is non-poisonous and absolutely safe to handle. It will not injure the tenderest growth.

Lemon Oil—Plants should be dipped in a solution of suitable strength. While it kills all scale insects, it is not injurious to the most tender plants.

Lime-Sulphur Solution—Lime unslaked, 20 pounds; sulphur, ground, 16 pounds, water to make 50 gallons. Place 8 to 10 gallons of water in an iron kettle over a fire, and when it reaches the boiling point, add the sulphur and mix thoroughly; then add the lime, which will immediately produce a violent boiling. From time to time add a small quantity of water as needed to prevent boiling over or burning. The sulphur gradually goes into solution, and the mixture, at first thick and pasty, becomes thinner and thinner, changing in color through several shades of yellow. After boiling at least one and a half hours, the mixture should be diluted to the proper amount by the addition of sufficient hot water. If a suitable boiler is not convenient, the mixture may be more economically cooked in barrels or tanks by the use of steam.

Thomsen Chemical Company's Lime-Sulphur Solution is recommended for the treatment of the San Jose scale, as the lime-sulphur treatment is superior in many ways to the other remedies. Write us for prices.

Naphtha Soap and Nicoticide—One ounce of soap and one-quarter ounce of Nicoticide to each gallon of water. It is advisable to have the water at 100 degrees Fahrenheit. This is an excellent spray for red spider.

Paris Green—Actively poisonous. Add 4 ounces of paris green, 1 pound of fresh lime, to 50 gallons of water. Paris green and bordeaux mixture may be applied together without the action of either being weakened.

Pyrethrum—One ounce of the "Bubach" powder added to 2 gallons of cold water, for any plant used for food, as this is non-poisonous.

Scalecide—One per cent solution of scalecide or 1 per cent prepared lime-sulphur solution will eradicate red spider.

Tobacco, 1 pound; boiling water, 2 gallons; strain when cool. It is very effective when used as a spray against flea beetles, aphides (plant lice).

White Hellebore, 1 ounce; water, 3 gallons. Effective as a spray for rose slugs.

SPRAYING.

We cannot be too emphatic in impressing on the horticulturist to spray his fruit trees and grape vines if he desires good fruit. Follow directions carefully. Experiments frequently result disastrously. Careless spraying will result in loss of fruit and sometimes the trees. Every fruit grower should purchase a spraying apparatus; it can now be had for a small sum. Be careful in keeping your solution continually stirred. The best time for spraying is late in the afternoon or during cloudy weather, except with kerosene emulsion; this should be used on bright, shiny days. (We recommend the Gould Pumps. Write us for prices on these; we can save you money.)

Other scale insects, of which there are several species, such as cherry scale, pecan scale, obscure scale on shade trees, can be controlled during the winter months by use of lime-sulphur or. soluble oil, or during summer months by spraying with kerosene emulsion or sulpho-tobacco soap.

NOTE—If your trees are infested with any insects or fungous diseases, send infested portion to your Experiment Station, your State Entomologist, or the United States Entomologist at Washington, D. C.

KILLS
Sulpho-Tobacco Soap.
INSECTS

Larkins Sulpho-Tobacco Soap gives best results in quickly exterminating all insect life on plants and flowers, in and out of doors. Effectively destroys squash and potato bugs, currant worms, lice, green fly, mealy bug, red spider, etc. Unexcelled for spraying shrubs. fruit trees and vines. This popular insecticide never fails to give satisfaction. It is cheap, clean, harmless and non-injurious to the tederest growth. You cannot afford to be without Sulpho-Tobacco Soap if you desire to be successful in plant culture. A trial will give highly gratifying results. We have discontinued handling anything smaller than the 10-pound size. By express, $3.00.

P. J. BERCKMANS CO.

Special Southern Evergreen Lawn Grass, "Fruitland Mixture"

IF YOU WANT A BEAUTIFUL LAWN THIS WINTER, TRY OUR "FRUITLAND MIXTURE."

For a number of years we have tested many grasses to determine which ones would stand best in the South. We have finally succeeded in obtaining one, our "Fruitland Mixture," which has given most satisfactory results, and we have not yet seen a better lawn grass for this section than our mixture produces. It is composed only of such grasses as have exhibited the greatest heat and drought-resisting qualities. These grasses are most carefully blended, resulting in a mixture that stands our hot weather better than any evergreen lawn grass that we have been able to obtain. Of course, during periods of intense heat and drought, the "Fruitland Mixture," as well as all other evergreen lawn mixtures, will burn out more or less. During the hot, dry periods use a lawn sprinkler or hose and nozzle after sunset. Lawns are frequently injured by using the hose and putting on the water with too great force, especially when the sun is shining. All of our seed has been re-cleaned, is strictly free from weeds, and of high germination. During prolonged droughts it pays to water daily instead of only periodically. Grass, when artificially watered, requires that this be repeated regularly.

A Fruitland Mixture Lawn.

How to Make a Lawn—The ground should be first thoroughly broken up with a plow as deep as possible. If the area cannot be plowed, then spade it up carefully and thoroughly, applying a liberal amount of well-rotted stable manure. Incorporate this thoroughly with the soil. Apply 7-7-6 fertilizer (7 per cent phosphoric acid, 7 per cent nitrogen, and 6 per cent potash) at the rate of 500 to 1,000 pounds to the acre, the quantity applied depending upon the fertility of the soil, or an application of sterilized sheep manure (which produces no weeds), at the rate of 1,000 pounds per acre, produces quick growth. Rake it well and level off the ground. When the surface has been raked perfectly smooth, the seed should be sown broadcast at the rate of 60 to 75 pounds to the acre (a space 210 x 210 feet). Rake lightly, barely covering the seed, then roll. If the space is too small for rolling, or if you do not possess or cannot procure a roller, devise some means of tamping or firming down the soil. In Spring a top-dressing of bone meal should be applied. If the weather is dry at the time of seeding, and there is no prospect of rain, water the lawn with a lawn sprinkler or with a nozzle on the end of a hose, regulating the flow so it will fall lightly on the ground. When the weather is very hot and dry do not mow the lawn as frequently or as closely as when weather conditions are more favorable. A light re-seeding on established lawns each Autumn will take care of the bare spots and will insure a good, substantial turf. By following these directions, no trouble should be experienced in obtaining and keeping a perfect lawn.

NOTE—The best period for making a lawn is from September to December. The earlier in the fall the better.

PRICES OF "FRUITLAND MIXTURE."

5 lbs.	$ 1.50
10 lbs.	2.50
15 lbs.	3.25
50 lbs.	10.00
100 lbs.	20.00

Spray Pumps

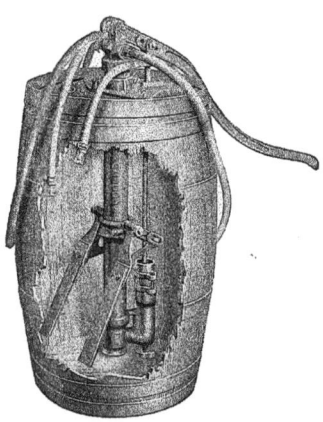

We can ship promptly from Augusta the following Gould's Spray Pumps: "Bordeaux" No 1129, "Pomona" No. 1100, "Monarch" No. 1500; also hose, nozzles, couplings and bands.

The "Pomona" pump is the most durable barrel sprayer. It is very powerful and will supply 4 leads of hose and 8 nozzles. The "Bordeaux" is placed in bucket, with foot-hold on outside. This is the best small pump made. The "Monarch" is the best high-grade sprayer for large orchards. We recommend the pumps made by the Gould Manufacturing Company. Write us for descriptive catalogues and special prices.

Pomona Pump No. 1100

Bordeaux Pump No. 1129.

AUGUSTA, GEORGIA.

Fruit Department

Apples

Varieties of European or northern origin, that mature their fruit in summer or fall, often prove as satisfactory and profitable in the South as those which have originated here; but the kinds that are most dependable for fall and winter use in that part of the southern states south of the Piedmont region are mainly seedlings that have been introduced by southern nurserymen.

Northern winter varieties seldom hold their fruit after the month of August in the section of country above referred to; but many of these northern varieties are grown most successfully in the Piedmont section, as also are many of the varieties native to the South.

Clay or clay loam is the best soil for growing Apples. The land should be plowed well and deep before setting the trees. It should, of course, be well drained and kept thoroughly cultivated. Too much emphasis cannot be put on the importance of drainage; recent investigation has shown that a surplus of water in the orchard produces fruit of an inferior quality and flavor. The expense of tiling or ditching is not to be compared with the profits that are received from an orchard that it properly drained and cultivated.

All of our Apples are budded or grafted on whole seedling stocks. We do not use pieces of roots for our propagation. Our Apples are unusually thrifty and vigorous.

Plant Apple trees 25 to 40 feet apart, each way, according to soil.

PRICES OF TREES, except where noted:	Each	10	100	1000
Standard, 2 year, 5 to 6 ft., extra heavy, well-branched	$0.30	$2.50	$17.50	$150.00
Standard, 1 year, 5 to 7 ft., extra heavy whips and partly branched, or 2 year, 4 to 5 ft. branched	.25	2.00	15.00	125.00
Standard, 1 year, 4 to 5 ft., whips and partly branched	.20	1.50	12.00	100.00

MARGARET, Early Red Margaret; Southern Striped June. Small to medium; rather flat; skin yellow, with dark red stripes; subacid and of high flavor. Ripens June 20; lasts until July 20.

May Pippin, White June Eating. Small, yellow; good quality; last of May.

RED ASTRACHAN, Red Ashmore; Early Rus, etc. Large; yellow, nearly covered with crimson, and fine bloom; juicy, crisp, acid; a beautiful fruit. Tree a thrifty and fine grower; excellent and profitable. Ripens end of May and continues through June.

RED JUNE, Carolina Red June, etc. Medium conical; deep red; juicy. Very productive. June 15 to end of July.

SIMMONS' RED. Large; orange, nearly covered with red; flesh yellow; sugary; good flavor; quality very good. Ripens June to September.

YELLOW TRANSPARENT, White Transparent, Grand Sultan, etc. Medium; yellow; good quality. A productive, excellent and popular variety. Tree of dwarfish habit. Bears young. June.

Kansas Queen.

Summer Apples.

Varieties for Market Orchards in Capitals.

COFFMAN. Summer Red; Coffman June. Medium large, roundish oblong; greenish yellow, striped and splashed with red, with white dots; flesh white, juicy, of good quality. An improvement on Red June. The tree is an upright grower. Last of June.

CAROLINA WATSON. Very large oblate-conical; green, striped with dull red, with a dull red cheek; sweet, crisp and very fragrant. Exceedingly prolific, and a good market fruit. Beginning of July.

EARLY HARVEST. Early June-Eating; Yellow Harvest. Medium to large; bright yellow; tender, juicy, well flavored. An excellent home-market apple; invaluable in any orchard. June 5, and lasts two or three weeks.

HORSE, Haas; Summer Horse; Yellow; Red or Green Horse, etc. Large; green; acid. Good for cooking and drying. Known everywhere. A very productive variety. July and August.

Hominy, Sops of Wine. Medium; red; very juicy, subacid. July.

KANSAS QUEEN. Large; yellow, nearly covered with crimson; good quality. Very reliable, productive, and a good market variety. Succeeds well on light, sandy soils. June to August.

Autumn Apples.

Varieties for Market Orchards in Capitals.

Bietigheimer, Red Bietigheimer. Large to very large; roundish; ground color pale cream nearly covered with purplish crimson; flesh white, firm, subacid; an early and heavy bearer. Ripens in September.

BONUM, Magnum Bonum. Medium; deep crimson; firm, tender, juicy, mild, subacid. September to October.

CAROLINA GREENING, Southern Greening; Yellow, or Green Crank; Southern Golden Pippin; Green Cheese. Medium; green or yellow; crisp, subacid; fine flavor. Compact grower and prolific. September.

Carter Blue, Lady Fitzpatrick. Originated in Alabama; large, roundish oblate; greenish, washed and striped with dull red, and covered with a blue bloom. Flesh yellowish white; crisp, sweet, rich, aromatic. Very good; a fine grower. September to November.

EQUINETELEE. Bachelor; King; Iola, Ne Plus Ultra; Byers; Buckingham; Kentucky Queen. Very large, oblate; yellow, with bright red cheek and crimson stripes; flesh yellow; subacid; very rich and juicy; a magnificent fruit. Ripens end of September and lasts until November. Tree compact and a vigorous grower; bears young.

9

P. J. BERCKMANS CO.

FALL PIPPIN, Hubbardson's Nonsuch; Pound Pippin; York Pippin, etc. Very large, bright yellow; flesh tender, juicy, subacid; quality best; valuable for market or table. September to October.

GRIMES, Grimes' Golden. Medium round, oblate; skin yellow, with small dots; flesh yellow, crisp; rich, subacid; very good. October.

HARGROVE, Originated in Haywood County, North Carolina. Above medium to large; oblate; golden yellow with a bright carmine cheek; flesh, crisp, white; excellent flavor; subacid; quality best; an excellent market sort. October to November.

MRS. BRYAN. Origin, Walker County, Georgia. Very large; orange-red; quality best. Maturity, September and October. An exceedingly handsome fruit, and becoming very popular in many sections.

PINE STUMP. Large; oblate; dark crimson; flesh yellow, crisp, sugary; good flavor. August and September. A very showy fruit. Tree spreading, vigorous and productive. One of the best varieties for the Piedmont section of Georgia, South Carolina and North Carolina.

WALLACE HOWARD. Very large; conical; deep orange-red, with a few crimson stripes; flesh brittle, sugary and highly flavored; quality best. A very showy fruit. October.

Winter Apples.

Varieties for Market Orchards in Capitals.

ARKANSAS BLACK. Large; dark red; flesh yellow; very good; subacid; good keeper; late.

BLACK WARRIOR. Above medium; green; quality best; fine keeper and first-class in every respect; prolific. October.

BEN DAVIS, New York Pippin; Thornton of Southern Alabama. Medium; oblate; greenish yellow, with a crimson cheek; subacid; fair quality. Keeps well.

Bismarck, Prince Bismarck. From New Zealand; has been fully tested in Europe and United States. Enormously productive; bears very young; quality good. Late fall and winter. Tree dwarf; is largely grown in pots for decorative purposes.

Blythe, Crab. A native of Richmond County, Georgit. Fruit sometimes two and one-half inches in diameter, an early and profuse bearer; a splendid keeper.

DELICIOUS. A remarkably popular variety in the West. Fruit large, nearly covered with dull dark red; fine grained. crisp, juicy; quality best; a splendid keeper and shipper; vigorous grower.

PORT, Fort's Prize. Medium size; deep crimson with pure white dots, and fine russet deepening towards apex and cavity; flesh white, crimson; good flavor; an excellent keeper; an attractive and reliable market sort; bears early; a vigorous grower; originated in Habersham County, Georgia, by Col. J. P. Fort.

GANO, Black Ben Davis; Red Ben Davis; Peyton. Roundish; oblate; large; color deep, dark red; flesh yellowish white; mild; subacid. Quality good, and a profitable market variety.

Haywood. A seedling of Hoover; yellow and dark crimson cheek; flesh white; subacid; good quality. Maturity, October. Compact growth.

Hewes, Hewes Virginia Crab. Small, dark red; regular and profuse bearer; valuable for cider. October to March.

Horn, North Carolina Vandevere. Medium; flat or conical; here and father south, dark crimson; farther north, green, with red cheek; juicy; rich. Ripens in November and keeps until March; tree an open grower; productive.

King, Crab. A native of Richmond County, Georgia. Fruit lemon yellow with bright carmine cheek; very showy; excellent for preserving; a very reliable and prolific variety; a fine keeper

KINNARD, Kinnard's Choice; Red Winter Cluster. Medium, obconical; yellow ground almost entirely covered with red; flesh yellow, crisp, tender, juicy, rich, subacid; very good; an excellent and reliable market variety; most prolific; an early bearer. Recommended most highly for the Piedmont section.

Mangum, Carter; Gully. Medium; red striped; flesh firm; juicy and well flavored. Ripens in October, and keeps well; productive, vigorous, compact grower.

PARAGON, Mammouth Black Twig. A Tennessee seedling with the combining good qualities of Winesap and Limbertwig; fruit very large, yellow striped red, subacid; medium to late.

Romanite, Broad River; Southern Romanite. Round, conical; small; yellow and red with blush cheek; flesh, juicy, yellow, sub-acid; very good; very late, an excellent keeper; prolific

ROME, Rome Beauty, Royal Red, Phoenix, etc. Large; yellow and bright red; medium quality; moderate grower; a good bearer; an excellent market sort. Ripens in October. Keeps well.

ROYAL LIMBERTWIG. Large; oblate; pale yellow; striped red; flesh yellow, rich and juicy; productive. Ripens in October, and will keep until the following summer. Cannot be classed as of first quality, but is yet the most popular winter variety we cultivate. Profitable market variety.

SHOCKLEY, Waddell. Hall, Sweet Romanite. Medium; conical; always regular; yellow, with a bright crimson cheek; flesh firm; sweet or subacid, with some flavor; trees very erect, vigorous, exceedingly productive; ripens in October and will keep until the following summer. Cannot be classed as of first quality, but is yet the most popular winter variety we cultivate. Profitable market variety for the South.

STAYMAN WINESAP, Stayman. A seedling of Winesap. Dark red; flesh firm, fine grained, crisp, subacid; quality best. Strong grower.

STEPHENSON, Stevenson's Winter; Stevens' Winter, etc. Medium to large; green, covered with brown; flesh firm, juicy and spicy. A regular bearer, and keeps until April. The tree is a fine grower.

TERRY, Terry's Winter. Originated in Georgia; medium size; subacid; red; best quality. An excellent market variety. Most prolific. November 1st.

WINESAP, Holland's Red; Winter Winesap, etc. Small to medium; red; vinous; quality very good. A good keeping apple

WINTER QUEEN, Poorhouse; Winter Green. Large; roundish; oblate; pale yellowish green; russet spots; flesh yellowish moderately juicy; mild; subacid; very good. Tree vigorous, compact grower. This is a valuable addition to our varieties, as it is an exceptionally good shipper and keeper. Ripens last of October.

YATES Red Warrior. Small, dark red, dotted with small white dots; flesh yellow, firm, juicy and very aromatic. Very heavy bearer and good keeper.

YORK IMPERIAL, Johnson's Fine Winter; Shepp, etc. Medium; whitish, shaded crimson; flesh yellow, crisp, juicy and subacid; very good. A profitable market variety for the upper sections. October.

NOTE.—Nearly all winter Apples commence to be in eating condition here in October, and if properly taken care of in a cool, dry room, free from frost, the larger number can be kept through the winter.

Crab Apples.

Siberian Varieties.

The flowers as well as the fruit are exceedingly ornamental. The trees are heavy and early bearers. The fruit is desirable for preserves, jelly, etc.

PRICES OF TREES: Each   10   100
Standard, 2 year, 5 to 6 ft., extra heavy, well branched......$ .30 $2.50 $17.50
Standard, 1 year, 5 to 7 ft., extra heavy whips and partly branched, or 2 yr. 4 to 5 ft., branched .... .25 2.00 15.00
Standard, 1 year, 4 to 5 ft., whips and partly branched .... .20 1.50 12.00

Golden Beauty, Golden Beauty Crab. A crab of medium size; fruit beautiful, golden-yellow; keeps well; exceedingly ornamental.

Large Red, Red Siberian Crab. Roundish, ovate; bright red on a light-yellow ground; flesh acid; very ornamental.

Transcendent, Transcendent Crab. Fruit sometimes two inches in diameter; yellow striped with red; fine for preserving and jelly; tree a vigorous and quick grower; very ornamental.

AUGUSTA, GEORGIA.

Apricots

Apricots give the best results when planted in a situation where they are protected from the north and west by buildings or trees. The Apricot is one of the most delicious fruits grown; therefore a little extra care should be given in protecting the blooms from late spring frosts. A smudging on nights when frosts impend will save the fruit. The trees, when planted in orchards, seldom last long here unless protected by surrounding timber or tall growing fruit trees. As the Apricot is particularly susceptible to the attack of the curculio, the fruit should be sprayed the same as peaches. The trees must be planted in high, well-drained ground, and must have clean cultivation. The period of maturity extends from the beginning of June to the end of July.

PRICES OF TREES: Each   10
   5 to 7 feet, extra heavy $0.50 $4.00
   4 to 5 feet, branched 35   3.00

AMBROSE. Large, rounded, early; skin deep yellow; flesh sugary and juicy; quality best. Middle June.

EARLY GOLDEN, Dubois. Fruit small, rounded; oval; skin smooth, pale orange; moderately juicy and sweet; very good flavor. Early June.

MOORPARK, Dunmore; Temple's; DeNancy, etc. Fruit large; skin orange; brownish red on sunny side; flesh bright orange; freestone; juicy; rich and luscious flavor. Very productive an unusually hardy variety, having produced fine crops as far north as Idaho. Late June.

ROMAN, Transparent; Grosse Germine, etc. Fruit medium-sized; skin pale yellow, sometimes dotted with a few red spots; flesh dull yellow, soft, rather dry; one of the largest growing and hardiest Apricot trees.

Figs

This fruit adapts itself to a wide range of soils and climates. By protecting the plants during winter some varieties have been successfully grown in the state of New York.

The canning of Figs for commercial purposes is gradually extending throughout the South. The supply of preserved and canned Figs is never equal to the demand. In some sections fresh Figs are also being successfully shipped to markets a distance of four or five hundred miles. The fruit must be carefully handled, and it should be packed in strawberry baskets.

The trees should be planted 12 to 18 feet apart, according to character of soil, and they should be trimmed so as to admit plenty of light and air into the center of the tree. Figs bear early, and the ripening period covers the season from June until November

PRICES OF TREES: Each   10   100
   2-year, heavy $0.30 $2.50 $20.00
   1-year, heavy 25   2.00   17.50

BLACK ISCHIA, Blue Ischia, etc. Fruit is of medium size: skin blue-black, with crimson pulp and of good quality; tree moderate bearer. Not so hardy as Green Ischia.

BROWN TURKEY. Medium; brown; sweet and excellent; very prolific. Most reliable for field-culture. One of our hardiest varieties.

BRUNSWICK, Madonna; Broughton, etc. Very large; violet; pulp thick; quality good; productive and hardy.

CELESTE, Sugar; Celestial, etc. Medium; pale violet; with bloom; sweet and excellent; prolific. Hardiest of all Figs.

GREEN ISCHIA, White Ischia. Medium to large; green; crimson pulp; excellent; prolific; rather late, but bears continually until frost.

LEMON. Fruit medium to large, flattened, slightly ribbed; yellow; flesh white; sweet; early. Strong grower and very prolific. A favorite for canning.

MAGNOLIA, Dalmation. Very large; greenish-amber; quality good; productive, but very tender; gives best results in Texas.

Nectarines

Require the same culture as the peach. The fruit, having a smooth skin, is very liable to the attacks of the curculio and brown rot, and must be sprayed according to directions on page 5. They ripen through July and part of August.

PRICES OF TREES: Each   10
   1-year, 5 feet and up, extra heavy $0.40 $3.50
   1-year, 4 to 5 feet 25   2.00

COOSA...Fruit large, red; flesh white; an excellent variety; originated in North Georgia.

ELRUGE. Red, mottled darker.

VICTORIA. Medium; purple, with brown cheek. July.

VIOLET, Early Violet. White, with blush cheek; flesh tender, juicy and of good flavor.

WHITE, New White. The fruit is produced early in the season, and is large, with a pure white skin; flesh is tender, juicy, with a vinous flavor.

Peaches.

PRICES OF TREES, EXCEPT WHERE NOTED: Each   10   100   1000
   1-year, 5 feet and up, extra heavy $0.25 $2.00 $15.00 $100.00
   1-year, 4 to 5 feet, heavy .... .15   1.25   10.00   70.00
   1-year, 3 to 4 feet, stocky .... .10   1.00   8.00   60.00
   1-year, 2 to 3 feet, stocky, mostly whips 75   6.00   40.00

Varieties for Commercial Orchards in Capitals. Dates of maturity given for latitude of Augusta, Ga., except when noted.

P. J. BERCKMANS CO.

Picking Peaches in Berckmans Brothers' Orchard, Mayfield, Georgia.

A well-drained, sandy loam with a clay subsoil is an ideal soil for the Peach. But the Peach has the faculty of adapting itself to almost any soil, provided it is well drained. Peaches, if planted in sour land, will probably die before reaching the bearing stage. All Peach lands should be tested for an excess of acidity, and if such acidity exists, the soil should be corrected by an application of lime. Always plant a 1-year tree. Cut the tree back to 18 inches and plant 18x18 or 20x20 feet. It is best to have a low-headed tree. In the spring, after the growth has started, remove all but three branches, and let these be distributed so that the tree will be well balanced. For the first two years fertilize with well-rotted stable manure, or a mixture of one part of cotton seed meal or bone meal to two parts of 16 per cent acid phosphate by weight. Apply 1½ to 2 pounds of this mixture to each tree. After the third year, avoid nitrogenous fertilizers, and use a fertilizer containing a good percentage of bone phosphate and potash and a small percentage of nitrogen.

Prune every year by cutting off one-third of the previous year's growth. The head of the tree should be broad and open, so as to allow free circulation of light and air. Never plant newly cleared woodlands; such lands should be cultivated for at least two years before setting the trees; otherwise wood-lice will injure them.

In preparing orchard land, plow as deeply as possible and then subsoil. Dig holes two feet square; better yet, use dynamite for making the holes. Cowpeas, soy beans or velvet beans are excellent crops for planting between the trees; it is best to drill in two feet apart, leaving four or more feet on each side of the trees, so as to have ample room for cultivation. Cultivate frequently, and in the late fall or early winter turn under the cover-crop. When the orchard begins to bear, it should have clean cultivation, but as soon as the fruit is harvested, drill in peas for cover-crop, and turn this under as above directed.

In fall it is always advisable to sow a cover crop, such as Clover, Vetch or Rye. This cover crop should be turned under in early spring.

Peaches, Freestone.

Alexander. Above medium; highly colored in clay soils; less so in light soils; flesh greenish white; very juicy, vinous and of good quality; adheres to the stone. Matures from May 20 to June 10. Remarkably prolific and bears very young. In many sections the fruit has proved to be a profitable variety for home use and market.

Angel. For Florida and sub-tropical sections only. Large; roundish; slightly pointed; skin yellow, highly washed with red; flesh white, juicy, fine flavor; seedling of Peen-to; ripens in North Florida June 20.

ARP. Arp Beauty. Yellow mottled crimson; very good; semi-cling; desirable variety; ripens June 15th.

BELLE, Belle of Georgia. Very large; skin white, with red cheek; flesh white, firm, and of excellent flavor; very prolific; excellent shipper. Tree a rapid grower. July 5 to 20.

BRACKETT. (Named by us in honor of Col. G. B. Brackett, Pomologist, U. S. Department of Agriculture, Washington, D. C.) After experimenting with the best named varieties, we have finally succeeded in securing in the Brackett a Peach which fills a long-felt want. Before disseminating this valuable Peach, we gave it a thorough trial for several years, and it has come up to our most sanguine expectations. Its period of ripening commences just at the close of the Elberta season. The fruit is a perfect freestone; large to very large, oblong, with sharp apex and shallow suture; color orange-yellow, washed red and mottled deep carmine, with a very dark carmine cheek; flesh deep yellow, juicy, highly flavored and of the best quality. This Peach is evidently a cross between Shock and Chinese Cling. It stands shipping well and promises to be a most popular variety. Make your reservations now.

	Each	10	100	1000
1 yr. 5 ft. and up, extra heavy	$0.40	$3.00	$25.00	
1 yr. 4 to 5 ft., heavy	.30	2.00	20.00	$150.00
1 yr. 3 to 4 ft., stocky	.20	1.75	15.00	125.00

BERENICE. Chinese Strain. Originated by the late Dr. L. E. Berckmans in 1877. Large to very large; yellow mottled with dark crimson; flesh yellow, melting, juicy, rich; in point of excellent quality it is superior to any yellow peach of its season. A popular shipping variety in sections where it is known. After giving this variety a thorough trial for many years we have nothing equal to it at the same season. Matures from end of July to middle of August.

CARMAN. Large; creamy white, with deep blush; skin tough, but flesh very tender and of fine flavor; prolific bearer. A most profitable and popular shipping variety. Ripens June 20 to July 1.

Chairs Choice. Large yellow; flesh very fine, heavy bearer; an excellent variety; matures August 15th to 30th.

CHAMPION. Large; skin creamy white, with red cheek; flesh rich and juicy. Ripens middle to last of July.

Climax. For Florida and sub-tropical sections only. A seedling of Honey, but larger; a heavy bearer; fruit of good appearance; round, slightly oblong; point recurved; pale yellow, washed red; flesh yellowish white, fine-grained, sweet. Ripens in North Florida June 25 to July 5.

12

AUGUSTA, GEORGIA.

Columbia. Pace; Yellow Indian; Tinley, etc. Large; dingy yellow and red stripes; flesh yellow, buttery, rich and sweet; quality best. End of July to middle of August.

Dr. Berckmans. Large, creamy-white, blush cheek; flesh white, melting, vinous, of the highest flavor; a seedling of Chinese Cling, but surpasses any variety of the same parentage, maturing at the same season. Matures middle to end of July.

EDE. Capt. Ede. Large, yellow; excellent quality; resembles Elberta but better flavor; ripens early in July.

ELBERTA. Large; yellow, with red cheek; juicy and of good flavor; flesh yellow. Supposed to be a seedling of Chinese Cling. Ripe middle of July. This is an excellent shipping variety.

Emma. Large, yellow with red cheek; flesh yellow, firm, juicy; best quality; ripens from July 25th to August 5th, follows Elberta.

Everbearing. Indian type. In some sections this Peach begins to ripen about July 1 to 15, and continues to produce successive crops until about the middle of September. Fruit varies in size from large to medium; is creamy white, mottled and striped with light purple and pink veins; oblong, tapering to the apex; flesh white, with red veins near the skin. Very juicy and of excellent flavor. Not recommended for commercial orchards, but for family use only.

Florida Gem. For Florida and sub-tropical sections only. A seedling of Honey, of large size; highly colored; roundish, oblong, pointed; sweet and juicy; red at the pit. A valuable market sort. Ripens July 1 to 10 in North Florida.

Ford's. Ford's Early. An excellent, large white flesh Peach of Chinese type; quality good, a heavy and reliable bearer; ripens June 15th.

Fox. Large; white, with red cheek; of good quality and flavor; regular bearer. A good peach. Middle of September.

Francis. Fruit medium large; almost red, with yellow cheek; yellow flesh; quality very good. Free stone. July 20 to August 1.

GREENSBORO. Origin, North Carolina. Ripens usually a week later than Alexander, but frequently with it, and is much larger and superior in every way. Round, sometimes elongated; flesh white; very juicy; of good quality; skin white, with red cheek; highly colored in the sun. A favorite and profitable early market sort.

HILEY. Early Belle. Large; white, with beautiful red cheek; flesh white; quality best Prolific bearer. Ripens June 25 to July 5. The best shipping variety of its season, which makes it very valuable.

Honey. Medium; oblong, with sharp recurved point, creamy-white, washed a mottled carmine; of honey sweetness; ripens June 15th to July 1st.

Imperial. A Florida variety very large; roundish; oblong; skin greenish yellow; red, with blush cheek; flesh white, juicy and of excellent flavor. Ripens in North Florida June 25 to July 5.

KENNESAW. Gov. Hogg; large white with beautiful cheek; flesh white, tender and juicy, highly flavored, red at pit, semi-cling; ripens June 20 to 25.

MAYFLOWER. An excellent new variety from North Carolina. Fruit round and entirely covered with red, Blooms late; very hardy. One week earlier than Sneed. This Peach is an acquisition.

Mountain Rose. Large white; washed with carmine; juicy, vinous, subacid; very good; ripens June 25.

Pallas. A seedling of Honey. Originated by the late Dr. L. E. Berckmans; resembles the parent but is much larger and more nearly round in shape flesh white, melting and vinous; ripens July 10.

Peen-to Free. For Florida and sub-tropical sections only. Fruit 2 to 2½ inches in diameter; very flat; Skin pale greenish white, with beautifully mottled red cheek; flesh finely grained; quality good. As this Peach colors some time before maturity, it is frequently gathered prematurely. Therefore it should be allowed to hang upon the tree until approaching full maturity to get the best fruit. Ripens in Florida from April 1 to May 10.

Picquet. Very large; yellow, with a red cheek; flesh yellow, buttery, rich sweet and of the highest flavor. Maturity from end of August to middle of September.

Red River. Medium to large; creamy-white, with crimson cheek; flesh white, very juicy; fine grained. vinous; quality very good; ripens middle to last of June.

Reeves. Large; oblong; skin deep yellow, with orange cheek; flesh juicy and buttery; very sweet; good. Ripens July 15.

Robert. Originated by the late Dr. L. E. Berckmans. Large, creamy-white, with crimson cheek and a few crimson stripes, flesh white slightly veined pink; melting, juicy and vinous; quality best; a desirable bearer; ripens August 15.

SALWAY. Large; dull yellow, mottled brownish red; flesh yellow, firm, but rather acid; fine flavor. August 15.

Skinner. Skinner's Choice. Originated at Augusta in 1915; medium to large; yellow almost entirely covered with red; flesh yellow, of fine flavor; reliable bearer; ripens July 1 to 10.

Slappey. Medium to large, clear, golden-yellow with dark cheek; flesh yellow, of fine quality; ripens July 5 to 10.

SNEED. Bowers, Peebles. Medium; creamy white with carmine mottling; flesh greenish white; juicy; semi-cling; quality fair. Ripens on an average six to eight days before Alexander.

St. John. Fleitas or Yellow St. John; May Beauty. Medium; roundish; orange yellow, with a deep red cheek; juicy, sweet and highly flavored; flesh yellow. Ripens end of June to July 10.

Summerour. Atlanta. Very large; rounded, deep yellow; flesh yellow, juicy, sweet and of good quality; ripens from middle to end of September. This peach fills a gap which has long been open in season of maturity; because it ripens after all good free stones are gone.

THURBER. Medium to large; skin white, with light crimson mottling; flesh very juicy, vinous, of exceedingly fine texture. Maturity July 1 to 10. A seedling of Chinese Cling. This variety seldom fails to yield a crop of fruit when other varieties fail, and is highly prized as a market sort in some sections.

Tornado. Fruit medium to large; skin reddish yellow; flesh yellow; good quality. Tree vigorous grower. Freestone. Ripens July 20.

VICTOR. Size below medium; creamy white, mottled light carmine; some faint dark stripes; flesh white, juicy, vinous; semi-cling. The quality is good, and is similar in many respects to Alexander. Ripens immediately after Sneed.

WADDELL. Of medium size; fine shape; skin greenish white; almost covered with red; flesh white and juicy; very prolific. A fine market sort.

Waldo. For Florida and sub-tropical sections only. Medium, roundish, oblong, bright yellowish-red; washed with carmine; flesh fine-grained, juicy and melting; ripens June 1.

WALLER. Originated by Waller Brothers, near Sparta, Georgia. Matures one week later than Elberta. Evidently of Crawford type. Large, but not quite averaging the size of Elberta; a very heavy and reliable bearer; skin yellow, but more than half covered with red; stringy, but of good quality.

Wonderful. Very large; deep yellow, with carmine blush; flesh yellow, firm, good. Ripens middle to last of August.

Peaches, Clingstone.

Albright. Large white, changing to light-orange; juicy, sweet, very good; ripens middle of October.

Bidwell's Early. For Florida and sub-tropical sections only. A seedling of Peen-to; creamy white with pale pink cheek; flesh very fine grained, buttery, melting and juicy; semi-cling; size medium to large; ripens in north Florida early in May.

CARSON. Originated in Hancock County, Ga. Medium to large, with pale yellowish ground completely overspread with light crimson, with deep carmine cheek; flesh white, very juicy, vinous, red near the stone. A sure and heavy bearer; a most desirable variety; ripens last of July.

P. J. BERCKMANS CO.

Demming. Large; oblong, with a protuberance; yellow, with red cheek; flesh yellow; red near the stone; juicy, vinous and good. Resembles Pineapple, but one month later.

Eaton. Medium; skin yellow, with occasionally a few pink spots; flesh yellow, sweet, juicy, apricot flavor. superior for canning. Middle of September.

GENERAL LEE. Improved Chinese Cling. Above medium; oblong; creamy white, with carmine wash; flesh very fine-grained; melting, very juicy, and of high flavor; quality best. July 1 to 10.

Hancock. Originated by Berckmans Brothers, Mayfield, Georgia. Very large; skin orange-yellow slightly mottled carmine; flesh fine-grained; flavor sweet; a vigorous grower and a reliable bearer; ripens August 10 to 15.

Heath Late White. White English; Eliza Thomas; Potter's September. Rauy; White Globe; Henrietta, etc. Large; oval, with sharp apex; skin creamy white; very seldom with any red; flesh pure white to the stone; juicy and sweet, with good aroma. Very popular for preserving. Ripens beginning of September.

Indian Blood. Large; dark claret, with deep red veins; downy; flesh deep red; very juicy. Middle of August.

Juno. Originated by Dr. L. E. Berckmans; very large; deep yellow, mottled with orange-crimson; flesh yellow, fine-grained, very juicy, vinous, subacid; quality best; ripens August 10 to 20.

KENT. Originated at Augusta, Georgia, and first disseminated by us; has been tested in many parts of the South, and in every one of these sections it has succeeded admirably; fruit large, slightly depressed at apex; skin greenish-yellow tinted carmine at apex and on cheek; flesh yellow, buttery and of exquisite flavor; skin very touch but peels very readily; an excellent shipper and we are sure will become one of the standard varieties for shipping. We recommend this variety unhesitatingly; ripens August 1 to 15.

Levy. Henrietta Cling. Fine cling; large size; skin deep yellow, shaded brownish red in the sun; flesh firm and juicy. Favorite variety in California.

Mealing. Originated by Dr. W. E. Mealing, North Augusta, South Carolina. Medium size; skin yellow, crimson on sunny side shading to deep orange; flesh firm, good quality; ripens last of August to middle of September.

Oriole. Originated by Dr. L. E. Berckmans. Large, yellow, rich, buttery. A yellow-fleshed Chinese cling; ripens August 15.

Pendleton. Very large; yellow; very good quality. Beginning of September.

Pineapple. Kennedy's Carolina; Allison; Largest Lemon, etc. Large; oblong, with a protuberance like a lemon; skin golden yellow, tinged with dark red; flesh yellow; slightly red at the stone; juicy; subacid; of excellent quality. Middle of August.

Plant. Very large; covered with red; flesh yellow, juicy, rich and sweet. An improved Orange Cling. Ripens from July 25 to August 10.

Sim's. Sim's Cling. Fruit large to very large, almost perfectly round; skin golden-yellow with fine blush on one side; flesh deep yellow of very fine texture; excellent flavor, pit small. In California this is considered the best variety for canning; ripens middle of August.

Stonewall Jackson. Almost identical with General Lee in size and quality, but ripens a week later; tree a more compact grower. July 10 to 20.

STINSON. Large; white, with red cheek; of very good flavor. The most profitable late Peach yet introduced for southern markets. Middle of October.

Pears

As a rule, Pears are most successfully grown in a very heavy, clay, or clayey loam, that has been well fertilized. If grown in sandy soil, coarse manure or litter should be worked into the soil. Mulching is of great benefit, and the orchard should be kept cultivated at all times.

This list of select varieties has been reduced to such as have been thoroughly tested and have proven valuable throughout the largest sections of the South. We grow Standard Pears principally, but can furnish Dwarf trees of a few varieties.

PRICES OF TREES: Each 10 100
Standard, 2 year, 5 feet and up, well branched $0.35 $3.00 $25.00
Standard, 1 year, 4 feet and up, whips or partly branched, or 2-year medium........ .25 2.00 17.50

Distance for planting: Standard trees 20 to 25 feet; Dwarf trees 15 to 20 feet apart each way.

Oriental Pears.

This type is peculiarly adapted to the South.

Garber. Resembles the Kieffer in size, appearance and quality, but matures here in August, and between the Le Conte and Kieffer. A thrifty grower and valuable variety.

Golden Russet. Japan Golden Russet. Large; almost globular; entirely covered with russet; firm, juicy; excellent for canning and preserving. A strong, vigorous grower.

Kieffer. Fruit large to very large; skin yellow, with a light vermillion cheek; flesh brittle; very juicy, with a marked musky aroma; quality good. Matures from September to October. Tree vigorous and very prolific. Begins to bear when four years old. If the fruit is allowed to hang upon the tree until the beginning of October, and then carefully ripened in a cool, dark room, it is a very attractive Pear.

Le Conte. Chinese Pear. Fruit large; pyriform; skin smooth; pale yellow; quality very variable; usually of second quality, but if allowed to mature slowly in a cool, dark room, its quality improves remarkably. Maturity from July 20 to end of August. Trees begin to bear when five years old.

Mikado. Large, yellow; flesh brittle; vigorous grower; good for cooking and preserving. Last of August.

Magnolia. Large, brownish-red; quality fair; matures later and keeps better than Kieffer. A desirable variety.

Smith. Almost identical with Le Conte in size, shape and quality, but a few days earlier.

European Pears.

SUMMER.

Alamo. Origin, Texas. Large; yellow, with bronze cheek. Tree a vigorous grower; bears young.

Bartlett. Large; buttery, melting, of rich flavor. Very popular. Ripens end of July and during August.

Archangel. St. Michael Archangel. Large; melting; very good; juicy; tree pyramidal; ripens in August.

Clapp Favorite. Resembles Bartlett, but ripens a few days earlier. Fine flavor. Tree a vigorous grower.

Doyenne. Doyenne d'Ete. Small, melting, very good; tree a medium grower; ripens early June.

Early Harvest. Good size and color; quality fair; very productive. Ripens in July.

Flemish Beauty. Large; melting; sweet; handsome. August.

Koonce. Medium to large; very handsome; juicy; sweet; very good. Tree a vigorous grower. Middle of June.

Lucrative. Belle Seigneur d'Esperen; Fondante d'Automme. Large; melting; delicious; fine grower; bears abundantly and regularly. End of July and August.

Marguerite. Petite Marguerite. Small; very early; an improvement upon Doyenne d'Ete. Ripens early in June.

Philadelphia. Large, melting, very good; middle of July.

Wilder. Small to medium; yellow, with dark red cheek; melting; sweet and very good. Beginning of June. Of vigorous and symmetrical growth. A valuable early market fruit.

14

PEARS—Continued.

WINTER AND AUTUMN.

Anjou. Beurre d'Anjou. Large; juicy; melting. A fine tree and regular bearer. September.

Angouleme. Duchesse d'Angouleme. Large; melting; juicy and well flavored. Vigorous grower and reliable bearer. August 15.

Clairgeau. Large, melting, sweet; a desirable variety; regular bearer; tree of stout growth. September and October.

Diel. Beurre Diel. Large; buttery; rich; vigorous grower. September.

La France. Resembles Angouleme, but a month or six weeks later. A desirable variety.

Langelier. Beurre Langelier. Medium, juicy, vinous and good; October and November.

Lawrence. Very large; melting; rich. Tree a remarkably fine grower. September and October.

Seckel. Of exquisite flavor; perhaps the standard quality in Pears. Tree a stout, slow grower. September.

Sheldon. Large; round; russety; first quality. Last of August.

Superfin. Beurre Superfin. Large; melting; subacid. Fine tree and regular bearer. August.

Dwarf Pears.

PRICES OF TREES	Each	10	100
2 years, 3 to 4 ft., branched	$0.30	$2.50	$20.00
1 year, 3 to 4 ft.	.25	2.00	15.00

Angouleme, Anjou, Superfin and Seckle. For descriptions see above.

Japan Persimmons (*Diospyros Kaki*)

The Japan Persimmon is thoroughly at home in the Cotton Belt. It does especially well in the Coast Region. Some varieties have succeeded in middle Kentucky and Virginia. We have also seen the trees growing successfully in southern New Jersey.

The tree is a vigorous grower and an early and most prolific bearer. In fact, the tree is apt to over-bear, and, therefore, the fruit must be properly thinned. The trees will succeed with little care or attention, but to get the best results they should receive the proper care and attention as to fertilization and cultivation.

This fruit is coming to the front for market purposes, and commands good prices, as it usually comes on the market in the fall and early winter. A careful selection of varieties will give fruit from August until frost. If the fruit is harvested before it is touched by frost, and house-ripened, the quality becomes greatly improved. For shipment the fruit should be packed in flat boxes with divisions, or in the standard six-basket carrier as is used for Peaches. Some varieties have dark flesh which are edible while the fruit is hard; whereas the light flesh varieties must be thoroughly matured before they can be eaten, as they are very astringent until fully ripened. The fruit of nearly every variety begins to color when half grown, but should be allowed to hang upon the tree until just before frost is expected, or in the case of early ripening varieties, when fully matured. Many of the late-ripening varieties can be kept until February. Some varieties will be seedless during certain years, and then again in other years they will contain more or less seeds: Furthermore, both round and pointed specimens are sometimes produced on the same tree.

PRICES OF TREES, EXCEPT WHERE NOTED:	Each	10	100
Budded and grafted, heavy, 5 to 7 ft., 2 year, 5/8-3/4 in. cal.	$0.50	$4.00	$35.00
Budded and grafted, 4 to 5 ft.	.30	2.50	20.00
Budded and grafted, 3 to 4 ft.	.25	2.00	17.50

Among. Yemon. Round; flattened; deeply ribbed; dark orange-red; 2½ to 3 inches in diameter; average weight, 6 ounces; flesh red; very sweet and sometimes edible while still solid.

Costata. Medium. Conical, pointed; 2⅛ inches long by 2⅝ inches in diameter. Skin salmon yellow; flesh light-yellow; astringent while solid, excellent when ripe. Ripens late; fine keeper; tree a rapid and upright grower. Luxuriant foliage.

Goshio. Very large; round; somewhat flattened; 3 to 3½ inches in diameter. Average specimen 10 ounces, and sometimes yields specimens 16 ounces in weight. Keeps late; flesh red; tree erect grower.

Hachiya. Imperial, Yomato, etc. Very large; oblong, with a blunt apex slightly ribbed; size 3 by 3¾ inches long by 3½ inches in diameter; flesh deep orange-red; astringent while solid, but sweet and very good when soft. Should be house-ripened and can be kept until March. The largest of all. Tree very vigorous and of tall growth.

Hiyakume. This is perhaps the most desirable of all the round, red-fleshed varieties, and as the fruit affects various shapes, it is known under many names such as Pound, etc. Fruit large, averaging 3 inches in diameter and 5 ounces in weight; usually flattened, but elongated forms are quite common upon the same branch; flesh bright orange-red. Keeps very late; must be soft before being edible. Tree of moderate height.

Okame. Mikado. Large; roundish, oblate, sometimes with quarter marks; point not depressed; skin orange-yellow, changing to brilliant carmine; flesh brownish red; good quality. Edible while solid.

Miyotan. Mazeli. Round, or slightly oblong; 2½ inches in diameter; skin deep orange-red; flesh usually deep reddish brown, but specimens of half-brown and half-red flesh are often produced on the same tree; keeps late. Brown specimens are edible while solid.

Tamopan. Big Grindstone. This valuable, new, vigorous variety was introduced by Mr. Frank N. Meyer, Agricultural Explorer of the Department of Agricul-

Japan Persimmon **Tsurunoko.**

JAPAN PERSIMMONS—Continued.

ture, Washington, D. C. In Japan this is considered the best of all persimmons. Fruit bright orange-red; skin thick and tough; flesh light colored; seedless; of excellent quality. Some without astringency and can be eaten while hard. The tree is a thrifty grower, and in Japan reaches a height of from 30 to 50 feet. If carefully handled, and by keeping the fruit at a cool temperature, it can be kept for several weeks.

PRICE OF TREES: Each   10
Strong trees, 4-5 feet $1.00 $8.00
Strong trees, 3-4 feet .... .50   4.00

Triumph. Originated in Florida, but grown from seed imported from Japan. Tomato shaped; medium size, imported 2¾ to 3 inches; bright red; skin smooth and bright red; flesh yellow, firm, and of fine quality. Very few seeds. Tree a strong and upright grower; very productive.

Tsurunoko. Stork Egg; Mino Kaki. Large; oblong; 2½ by 3½ inches; weight, 4 to 5 ounces, sometimes 10 ounces; skin bright red; some specimens covered with black at apex; flesh red; very good; keeps late. Edible only when soft. Foliage long and shiny; tree compact, of vigorous growth.

Zengi, or Zingi. Small; 1¾ to 2 inches in diameter; weight, 3 to 4 ounces. Flesh dark brown, with dark spots. Very sweet. Edible as early as middle of September, while still solid. Tree is a strong, healthy grower, producing fruit very freely.

Plums

PRICES OF TREES: Each   10   100
5 to 7 feet, extra heavy $0.40 $3.00 $25.00
4 to 5 feet .... .25   2.00   17.50

Distance for Planting, 15 to 25 feet apart, each way

Native Plums.

Hanson. American Type. Tree of average growth; fruit medium, globular, yellow overspread with red; skin thick; flesh yellow, juicy; quality good, very productive; ripens July 15.

Wild Goose. Chickasaw Type. Large, somewhat oblong; bright, vermillion red; juicy, sweet; good quality; cling; a very showy and profitable plum; ripens middle of June.

Japanese Plums.

Prunus triflora of botanists.
Prunus Japonica of pomologists.

Abundance. Yellow-Fleshed Botan. Round, with pointed apex, but varies from quite round to sharply pointed. Skin yellow, heavily washed purple-carmine and a darker cheek; flesh yellow, very juicy, subacid, with apricot flavor; quite firm; skin tough; clingstone; quality best; pit large. Maturity June 15 to July 5. We also have this variety under several names as received from Japan, all proving identical. One of the best early varieties, and valuable for northern and middle states. Carries well to distant markets. After fruiting this variety extensively for many years, we consider it the most desirable for shipping. Fruit should be thinned; otherwise the size is reduced and the quality is inferior.

America. Originated by Luther Burbank; fruit very large, glossy coral-red; flesh light-yellow; best quality; a very hardy and valuable sort; ripens last of June.

Burbank. In general characteristics, resembles Abundance, or Yellow-Fleshed Botan, slightly differing in foliage. Color cherry-red, mottled yellow; shape usually more globular; flesh, flavor and quality are identical, but its period of maturity here is from two to three weeks later, or middle to last of July. The tree is of very vigorous habit. Valuable also for northern states.

Chabot. Length, 2 to 2½ inches by 2 inches broad; yellow ground, nearly covered with carmine-red; flesh orange yellow; very solid; subacid; quality very good; clingstone. Maturity end of July. Identical with Bailey of several growers.

Combination. Originated by Luther Burbank. One of the best; an extra handsome, large, light-crimson Plum; of very best quality; flavor unsurpassed; nearly globular, uniform; flesh light-yellow; nearly free-stone; ripens June 5 to 15.

Douglass. Munson; Haytan-Kayo. Large, pointed, dark, purplish-carmine, with blue bloom; juicy, sweet; very good; a clingstone; a fine variety; July 20 to August 1.

Formosa. Originated by Luther Burbank; fruit very large, heart-shaped, light-cherry red; flesh pale yellow, unusually firm, sweet, rich and of a delightful flavor; ripens in July.

Gaviota. Originated by Luther Burbank; a deep, reddish purple; flesh yellow, sweet; pit very small; a beautiful variety; ripens last of July.

Kelsey. Large to very large, often seven to nine inches in circumference; large, heart-shaped; color greenish yellow overspread with reddish purple and blue bloom; flesh very solid, yellow, rich and juicy; excellent flavor; pit very small; semi-cling; matures from middle of July to end of August.

Kerr. Hattankio No. 2. Variable in shape; perfectly round and pointed specimens sometimes produced upon the same tree; skin yellow; flesh yellow, juicy, subacid; quality very good; clingstone; very prolific; ripens June 10 to 20.

Ogon. Medium to large, round, golden-yellow; flesh yellowish-carmine, subacid; freestone; vigorous grower; fine for preserving and cooking; ripens June 1 to 15.

Red Nagate. Red June, or Long Fruit. 1¾ by 1¼ inches, pointed; skin thick; purplish red, with blue bloom; flesh yellow, solid, somewhat coarse-grained, juicy, subacid, with Damson flavor; clingstone; quality good. Maturity 10th to end of June. Very prolific, showy and attractive in color. It ripens a week before Abundance, and is the earliest large-fruited market variety.

Rutland Plumcot. Originated by Luther Burbank; a cross between a Plum and an Apricot; the tree has long, pendulous branches; fruit large with a deep purple, velvety skin; flesh red with subacid flavor; excellent for cooking, jams and jellies.

Santa Rosa. Originated by Luther Burbank; fruit very large, deep purplish-crimson with a glaucous bloom; the flesh near the skin is purple blended with rosy scarlet, and pale amber near the pit, which is very small. It possesses a refreshing acidity and delightful aroma. A good grower, good bearer, keeps well; ripens middle of June.

Satsuma. Blood Plum; Yonemomo. Large; skin dark purplish red, mottled with bluish bloom; shape globular, or with sharp points; flesh firm, juicy, dark red or blood-color. Well-flavored and firm; quality very good; pit small. Unsurpassed in quality for canning. Maturity middle of July. Tree very vigorous. One of the most valuable varieties for this section, and adapted to the middle and northern states.

Wickson Plum.

16

AUGUSTA, GEORGIA.

PLUMS—Continued.

Terrell. A Florida seedling. A cross between a Japanese and Chickasaw Plum. Strong grower; fruit one and one-half to two inches in diameter; nearly round, slightly ribbed, reddish-yellow, mottled, covered with purple bloom; flesh reddish-yellow, sweet, juicy; good quality; clingstone. Highly recommended for Florida and Gulf Coast.

Wickson. Fruit large to very large; obconical; waxy white when half-grown, then the color gradually changes to pink and to dark crimson-purple; flesh very firm, yellow, juicy, subacid and highly flavored; pit small; clingstone; best quality. July 10 to 25.

European Plums.

The following varieties of Plums do best in the Piedmont section:

Clyman. A California seedling large, redish-purple; flesh firm: freestone, vigorous and a good bearer.

Giant Prune. The largest Prune known; fruit averaging one and one-half to two ounces each; retaining the good qualities of smaller varieties.

Lombard. Medium; violet red; juicy; good; hardy and productive; ripens early in July.

Shropshire. Of medium size; dark purple. Good for preserving. Thrives best in the Piedmont section. Very productive.

Quinces

These succeed best in strong, clay soils, in special localities, and in the Piedmount section. They can be grown in bush form. Being somewhat subject to leaf-blight, the trees should be sprayed with bordeaux mixture before the buds swell, repeating the spraying throughout the summer at intervals, as necessary. However, in some situations, Quinces seem to be free of blight.

PRICES, except where noted: Each   10   100
Strong, 3-year, grafted, 4 to 5 feet, branched........................$0.50 $3.50 $30.00
Strong, 2-year, grafted, 3 to 4 feet, branched........................ .40   3.00   25.00

Angers. A productive old variety. Fruit rather acid.   Each   10   100
3-year trees $0.25 $2.00 $15.00

Apple, or Orange. Large; round. Excellent late variety; bears abundantly.

Rea. Rea's Mammoth. A very large and fine variety of Apple Quince. A thrifty grower and productive. By some considered the best of all Quinces.

Meeche. Larger than Apple Quince. Ripens early.

Nut-Bearing Trees

Almonds.

Almonds are unreliable in most of the middle sections of the South; owing to their early blooming period the fruit is apt to be killed by late frost, unless the trees are protected. In some sections of the South the Almond is quite successfully grown.

PRICES: Each   10
1-year trees, 5 to 7 feet, heavy.........$0.40 $3.50
1-year trees, 4 to 5 feet................ .30   2.50

I. X. L. A desirable California variety. Sturdy, upright grower; nut large; soft shell; heavy bearer.

Nonpareil. Also called Extra. Tree of pendulous growth; a heavy and regular bearer. Shell thin; considered one of the best.

Princess. A soft-shelled European variety, grown for commercial purposes.

Sultana. Soft shell variety; one of the sorts mostly cultivated in Europe for commercial purposes.

Texas. Texas Prolific. Medium size; very plump; soft shell; a good bearer.

Chestnuts.

Large Spanish Chestnut. Nuts large; not so sweet as American, but command a ready sale. Does well in this locality. Bears early and freely.

PRICES: Each   10   100
2 to 3 feet, branched, stocky ..$0.25 $2.00 $15.00

Filberts.

European White. Will grow in almost any soil, and requires but little space. Nut oblong; very sweet. Suited to the Piedmont section.

PRICES: Each   10   100
3 to 4 ft., bushy $0.35 $3.00 $25.00
2 to 3 ft., bushy .... .25   2.00   17.50

Walnuts.

ENGLISH WALNUTS

(Thin-Shelled, or Maderia Nuts)

The English Walnut must be planted in rich, well-drained and preferably stoney soil. Do not plant in hard pan, heavy clays, or soils which are not properly drained. In some sections the English Walnut is successful. The trees we offer are all grown from the best French seed. Nuts large, oblong; shell very thin; of excellent quality, and the nut keeps sweet for a long time.

PRICES: Each   10   100
5 to 6 ft., extra heavy.........$1.00 $8.00
4 to 5 ft., very heavy .... .75   6.00 $50.00
3 to 4 ft., heavy .... .50   4.00   35.00
2 to 3 ft., heavy .... .35   3.00   25.00
18 to 24 in. .... .25   2.00   15.00

JAPANESE WALNUTS

The Japan Walnut succeeds from Massachusetts southward. It seems to be particularly successful in the southern states. The tree is very handsome; has a large, spreading top. It makes a useful as well as a very ornamental tree. At three years of age the tree commences to bear. The nuts are borne in clusters of from ten to twenty. The shells are moderately thick, but the kernels are very sweet. We offer two varieties.

PRICES: Each   10   100
4 to 5 ft., very heavy $0.50 $4.00 $35.00
3 to 4 ft., heavy .... .40   3.00   25.00
2 to 3 ft., heavy .... .30   2.50   17.50
18 to 24 in., heavy .... .25   2.00   15.00

Juglans Cordiformis. Nut bread; pointed; flattened; medium sized, somewhat resembling the shellbark hickory. If cracked longitudinally, the kernel can be removed entire.

Juglans Sieboldiana. Shaped like the butternut. Shell thicker than that of the English Walnut. A handsome tree; perfectly hardy in all parts of the country.

P. J. BERCKMANS CO.

Pecans

Where soil and climatic conditions are proper, it has been practically demonstrated that Pecan-growing is a paying investment; but only grafted or budded trees of well-known and meritorius varieties, should be planted, and these varieties should have the following qualifications: Large size, good flavor, thin shell, easy-cracking quality, and freedom from disease; furthermore, the purchaser should know that the trees are propagated from grafts or buds taken from good, bearing trees.

It is a well-established fact that some varieties of Pecans, the same as with other fruits, are adapted to certain localities, whereas the same varieties are not so good in other locations. It is not yet known which variety is adapted to the greatest number of localities. There are scores of varieties now cultivated and new sorts being advertised every year, but a half-dozen of the best tested and well-known sorts would be amply sufficient for any commercial grower.

Pecans should be planted from 40 to 60 feet apart, according to the soil. The Pecan will adapt itself to a great variety of soil—the rich, alluvial soil of the river bottoms, the high rolling land, and the sandy pine levels; but never set a Pecan in pipe-clay land or that which is not well drained, for if the land sours the trees will be killed or so badly injured that they will never give satisfactory results.

Some varieties of Pecans are hardy as far north as Iowa. Its natural distribution includes fifteen degrees of latitude. The trees can be safely transplanted as soon as they are thoroughly matured in the fall, and the transplanting can be safely done until March. It is a mistake to think that Pecans do not need cultivation. They must be cultivated and fertilized if you desire to get returns from the trees. The land between the rows can be planted for several years in cotton, peas, potatoes or vegetables. Stable manure, bone meal or high-grade commercial fertilizer are excellent fertilizers for Pecans.

When the Pecan reaches the bearing age the trees should have plenty of potash.

Pecan Tree.

As to the commercial value of nuts, this varies according to size and demand. Nuts running 30 to 50 to the pound wholesale from 30 to 60 cents per pound. The largest sizes bring fancy prices.

Pecans are long-lived. Budded and grafted trees, if well cared for, will bear at five years of age, but you cannot expect paying results before the trees are from seven to eight years of age. A ten-year-old tree should produce from fifteen to fifty pounds of nuts. If insects or fungous diseases affect the Pecan, see page 5.

Directions for Handling and Transplanting Pecans.

Take great care in preventing the roots of trees from becoming dry by being exposed to the weather. Keep the roots moist and covered at all times. When taking the trees to the field for setting, they must be carefully covered with moss, wet sacks or something similar, to protect them from drying out. This is important. Only one tree should be removed at a time, and this set at once in the hole previously dug. The hole must be at least two feet wide and of proper depth. Cut off the ends of all bruised or broken roots. Use a sharp knife for this; do not use an axe or hatchet. It has been practically demonstrated that it is advisable to cut off a part of the tap-root, as this causes the roots to throw out laterals. This will allow the trees to receive more food, and at the same time affords it a firmer hold upon the land. Place the tree in the hole about two inches deeper than it originally stood in the nursery row; fill the hole about half full with well pulverized top soil in which there is a proper proportion of well-rotted stable manure. If this is not available, use the proper amount of high-grade fertilizer. This must also be thoroughly mixed with the soil.

Pack the earth well about the roots of the tree—the firmer the better. Fill up the hole and pack the dirt well, but leave at least two inches of loose soil on top. If the soil is very dry, some water should be poured about the tree when the hole is partly filled. When the trees are more than four to five feet in height, the top should be cut back to within four feet of the ground. Do this after the tree is planted. Be careful not to break the eyes off the tree in handling. Keep them well cultivated and properly pruned.

We have had excellent results in planting Pecans with dynamite—one-half pound of dynamite placed four feet below the level is ample.

All our trees are budded or grafted on thrifty two and three year seedlings, and are, therefore, very hardy and satisfactory.

PRICES:	Each	10	100
5 to 6 ft., heavy	$1.25	$12.00	$110.00
4 to 5 ft., heavy	1.00	9.50	90.00
3 to 4 ft., heavy	.90	8.50	70.00
2 to 3 ft., stocky	.75	7.00	60.00

Frotscher. Very large, nuts averaging 45 to 50 to the pound. Shell very thin; can be cracked with the teeth; meat sweet and of fine quality, and can be removed entire from the shell. One of the best Pecans grown.

Jerome. Our stock is grown from the parent tree, which originated in Louisiana. This is a seedling of Pride of the Coast, but far superior to the parent. The tree is very healthy and vigorous; nuts very large; shell about the same thickness as Pride of the Coast. Good cracking quality and well filled. Runs 30 to 50 to the pound. For several years we inadvertently sent out this Pecan under the name of Pride of the Coast. The Jerome is unquestionably a very superior variety and a heavier bearer.

Schley. Medium to large; 1½ to 1⅞ inches long; oblong, slightly flattened; shell thin; plump, rich flavor; good grower; one of the best.

Stuart. Nut large to very large; 1¾ to 2⅛ inches long; oblong; shell of medium thickness, and of very good cracking quality; kernel full, plump, of best quality; flavor rich and sweet; a good grower; heavy bearer; excellent.

Van Deman. Nut large to very large; from ⅞ to 2⅛ inches in length, slender, pointed at both ends; shell of medium thickness; excellent cracking qualities; kernel full and plump; flavor good; vigorous grower; large foliage.

AUGUSTA, GEORGIA.

Small Fruits

Blackberries.

Cultural Directions—Blackberries thrive on almost any soil, but the most desirable is a strong loam, retentive of moisture, tending toward clay rather than sand, but it must be well drained at all times. Fertilizers containing a good proportion of potash are the most desirable; too much humus or nitrogen will induce a rank growth of wood at the expense of the fruit. As a preventive for rust, spray with copper sulphate during the fall and winter, and with bordeaux (4-6-50) during the spring and summer. The rows should be 6 to 8 feet apart, and the plants from 3 to 4 feet in the row, according to the character of the soil. If desired to cultivate both ways, set the plants in checks 6 to 7 feet each way. As soon as the fruiting season is past, remove the old canes; these should be burned at once. The young canes should be clipped off when they reach the height of about 2 feet; this will cause them to branch, and they will become self-supporting. Apply fertilizer during the late winter, and give shallow and constant cultivation.

Eldorado. Very hardy and vigorous. Berries large; borne in large clusters, and ripen well together; very sweet; no core. A heavy bearer, and valuable sort.
10 cents each; 75 cents for 10; $2.00 for 50; $3.00 per 100; $20.00 per 1,000

Mersereau. A most valuable variety. Fruit of immense size. Early and enormous bearer; very hardy.
10 cents each; 75 cents for 10; $2.00 for 50; $3.00 per 100; $20.00 per 1,000

Dewberries.

Cultural Directions—Use short, stout stakes, driven at the end of each row of canes, with a cross-piece 18 inches long nailed to each stake, 2½ to 3 feet from the ground. On the top, near each end of these cross-pieces, drive a stout nail, slanting toward the stake, upon which to catch a wire. Two lines of No. 14 galvanized wire, one on each side of the row, are fastened to one of the end stakes and run on the ground between the rows to the other end stake. These wires are now drawn as taut as possible and securely fastened to the other end of the row. The wires are now raised and caught in the nails, thus holding all the canes closely together in the row.

All Dewberries should be mulched to keep the berries from the ground.

Austin, Mayes. Fruit very large, subacid, vinous, but of second quality. Enormous bearer. The most productive market variety we have ever grown, and is 8 to 10 days ahead of any other. Strong and vigorous grower, and stands our hottest summers perfectly. Free from rust.
10 cents each; 50 cents for 10; $1.50 for 50; $2.00 per 100

Lucretia. One of the low-growing, trailing Blackberries. In size and quality it equals any of the tall-growing sorts. Hardy and very productive, with large, showy flowers. Fruit sweet and luscious; early.
10 cents each; 50 cents for 10; $1.50 for 50; $2.00 per 100

Raspberries.

Cultural Directions. The same as for Blackberries and Dewberries. These thrive best in a deep, moist, well drained soil; the lighter loams are best for the red and the heavy loams for the blackcaps. To make a success of Raspberries, the land should be able to withstand drought well. Cottonseed meal, pure ground bone, or fertilizers containing a good proportion of potash are best and should be liberally applied during the winter and early spring. To get the best results and keep the plants in vigorous condition, they must be mulched heavily with straw.

Columbia. Fruit resembles Shaffers; very large; purplish; vigorous and productive.
Each 10 50 100
Strong plants $0.10 $0.50 $2.00 $3.00

Cuthbert. Queen of the Market. This is the best and most reliable of the red-fruited varieties. Fruit large, red and of excellent quality, prolific bearer; ripens middle of May and continues for several weeks. Fine shipper.
Each 10 50 100 1000
Strong plants ..$0.10 $0.50 $1.50 $2.00 $15.00

Golden Queen. Fruit golden-yellow; similar in quality to Cuthbert, to which it is evidently a close relation. Its fine color attracts the eye. Prolific; withstands our summers.
Each 10 50 100
Strong plants $0.10 $0.75 $2.00 $3.50

Gregg. Blackcap. Very productive; large size.
Each 10 50 100
Strong plants $0.10 $0.50 $2.00 $3.00

St. Regis. Berries large, bright crimson; flesh rich; wonderfully prolific; bears early; produces fruit through a long period. We have given this a thorough trial and consider it one of the best Raspberries ever sent out.
Each 10 50 100
Strong plants $0.10 $0.75 $2.50 $3.50

Grapes. Native Varieties.

The varieties below described have been thoroughly tested by us. In addition we can supply a limited quantity of vines of several other good sorts. Our plants are strong and vigorous.

In transplanting Grapes, leave the main branch and cut this back to two or three eyes. The usual distance for planting Grapes is 10 by 10 feet. If you want to get good results from your Grapes, prune annually.

PRICES OF ASSORTMENT, OUR SELECTION OF VARIETIES:
10 strong vines in 10 best varieties for table use $1.00
100 strong vines in 10 best varieties for table use 8.00
Special quotations will be given for lots of 1,000 and upward.

FOR PURCHASER'S SELECTION. Not less than five vines of one variety will be charged at the rate for 10; not less than 40 vines of one variety will be charged at the rate for 100.

Agawam. Rogers' No. 15. Large; dark red.
10 cents each; 80 cents for 10; $5.00 per 100

Amber. Pale amber; long bunches; berry medium; sweet; fine flavor.
15 cents each; $1.25 for 10; $6.00 per 100

Brighton. Bunch medium; berry large, reddish; skin thin; quality best. An excellent early table or market Grape. Vigorous.
15 cents each; $1.25 for 10; $6.00 per 100

Catawba. Bunch and berry large; deep red, with lilac bloom; juicy, vinous and of musky flavor.
10 cents each; 80 cents for 10; $5.00 per 100

Concord. Bunch and berry very large; blue-black, with bloom; skin thin; cracks easily; flesh sweet, pulpy, tender; quality good. Very prolific and a vigorous grower. One of the most reliable and profitable varieties of general cultivation.
10 cents each; 80 cents for 10; $5.00 per 100

Delaware. Bunch compact; berry medium; light red; quality best; moderate grower, but vine very healthy; very prolific and more free from disease than any other variety. The most popular Grape grown; unsurpassed for table and for white wine.
15 cents each; $1.25 for 10; $6.00 per 100

GRAPES—Continued.

Diana. Bunch large, compact; berry large, reddish lilac; sweet; very productive. Ripens about August 15 to 25.
15 cents each; $1.25 for 10; $6.00 per 100

Elvira. Pale green; skin thin; sweet and juicy; one of the most reliable Grapes for the mountain regions.
10 cents each; 80 cents for 10; $5.00 per 100

Ives. Bunch very large; berry large; blue; skin thick; flesh pulpy, sweet, very musky; vigorous grower and prolific bearer. Very hardy and popular as a wine Grape.
10 cents each; 80 cents for 10; $5.00 per 100

Lindley. Bunch medium, loose; berry medium to large; color red; flesh tender; sweet; rich, aromatic flavor. Mid-season.
15 cents each; $1.25 for 10; $6.00 per 100

Lutie. Sweet; very pulpy; skin tough; quality fair, but a very hardy and valuable variety.
15 cents each; $1.25 for 10

Mary Wylie. Berry above medium, slightly amber tinted; highly flavored; flesh dissolving, vinous and delicate; quality best; skin thin.
15 cents each; $1.25 for 10

Massasoit. Rogers No. 3; bunch medium; rather loose; berry medium, brownish-red; tender and sweet.
15c each; $1.25 per 10; $6.00 per 100

Muscat of Alexandria. (European). Very large bunches; berry light yellow; delicate muscat flavor. A very popular variety for forcing under glass.
25 cents each

Moore's Diamond. Large; greenish white; juicy; little pulp and of very good quality. Yields abundantly; fruit perfect and showy. Ripens very early in July; the best very early white variety.
15 cents each; $1.25 for 10; $6.00 per 100

Moore's Early. Bunch medium; berry large, round; black, with heavy blue bloom; medium quality. Very early, desirable market sort.
15 cents each; $1.25 for 10; $6.00 per 100

Niagara. Bunch and berry large; greenish yellow; flesh pulpy, sweet, foxy. Its remarkable size and fine appearance give it much popularity as a market variety; vigorous and prolific.
10 cents each; 80 cents for 10; $5.00 per 100

Progress. Bunch large; berry medium, purple; pulp tender, vinous; an excellent table grape.
15 cents each; $1.25 per 10

Salem. Rogers' No. 53. A strong, vigorous grower; berries large, color of Catawba; thin skin; sweet and sprightly.
15 cents each; $1.25 for 10; $6.00 per 100

Worden. Resembles Concord, but is a few days earlier, and generally regarded as a better Grape.
15 cents each; $1.25 for 10; $6.00 per 100

Bullace or Muscadine Grapes.

(Vitis rotundifolia or Vulpina)

This type is purely southern, and is of no value for the northern or western states. Vine is free from all disease. The fruit never decays before maturity. The product is very large, and the cultivation reduced to the simplest form. Plant from 20 to 30 feet in a row; train on an arbor or trellis.

Strong, 2-year, heavy, transplanted vines, 20 cents each; $1.50 per 10; $12.00 per 100

Flowers. Bunches have from 15 to 25 berries; black, and of sweet, vinous flavor. Matures from end of September to end of October, or four to six weeks later than Scuppernong.

James. Berries very large; blue-black; in clumps of from 6 to 10; skin very thin; pulp tough, sweet and juicy, but not dissolving; quality very good. A showy variety. Ripens after Scuppernong.

Scuppernong. Berries large; seldom more than 8 to 10 in a cluster; color brown; skin thick; flesh pulpy, very vinous, sweet, and of a peculiar musky aroma. A certain crop may be expected annually. Vine is free from all disease and insect depredations. Fruit has never been known to decay before maturity. Wonderfully prolific. Popular wine Grape; wine, when properly prepared, resembles Muscatel.

Thomas. Bunches from 6 to 10 berries; berries slightly oblong, large, violet, quite transparent; pulp tender, sweet and of a delightful vinous flavor. Best of the type. Very little musky aroma. Makes a superior wine Grape. Matures middle to end of August.

Miscellaneous Fruits

Citrange

Citranges are products of Mr. Weber, of the United States Department of Agriculture, Washington, D. C. They are crosses of the Citrus trifoliata and the best varieties of Oranges in cultivation. In these crosses Mr. Weber has made it possible to produce fairly palatable Oranges in sections of the country where the mercury goes to zero. These Citranges have been tested for a number of years, and in this section it is seldom that the foliage is injured by the cold. The leaves are trifoliate, but of large size; thus showing the blood of the Citrus trifoliata and the Orange.

We offer strong, grafted plants of several named varieties as follows:

Morton, Rusk, Willet, etc.	Each	10
12 to 15 inch, branched	$0.50	$4.00

Orange.

Satsuma, or Oonshiu. So far this is the hardiest known edible Orange. It is of the Mandarin type. At Augusta it has stood a temperature of 12° above zero without injury. The trees are of drooping habit with broad, spreading heads; thornless; bears early. The fruit is of medium size, flattened like the Mandarin; color deep Orange, flesh tender and juicy; seedless; ripens at Augusta in September and October. All of our Satsumas are field-grown and grafted on Citrus trifoliata.

PRICES:
	Each	10	100
4 yrs., 4 to 5 ft., very bushy	$2.00	$15.00	
3 yrs., 3 to 4 ft., bushy	1.50	10.00	$80.00
2 to 3 ft., well branched	1.00	7.50	60.00
18 to 24 in., branched	.75	6.00	40.00
12 to 18 in., branched	.50	4.00	30.00

Elaeagnus edulis

AUGUSTA, GEORGIA.

Elaeagnus (*Japan Oleaster.*)

Elaeagnus edulis. (Longipes) Gumi fruit of the Japanese. A low-growing ornamental shrub. In early April produces very fragrant. reddish-yellow flowers which are immediately followed by bright red edible fruit, which is one-third of an inch in length; oblong, covered with minute white dots. This fruit will make an excellent jelly and marmalade; flavor is sharp, pungent, and rather agreeable; foliage light-green, silvery beneath. A beautiful ornamental shrub, almost evergreen.

PRICES: Each   10   100
2 to 3 ft., strong, bushy $0.50 $4.00
18 to 24 inches, bushy ...... .35   3.00 $25.00
12 to 18 inches, strong, well branched .... .25   2.00   17.50

E. Simonii. Simon's Oleaster. Fruit larger than Edulis; matures here in March. Owing to its early-blooming properties, the fruit is apt to be killed in this latitude by late frosts. The plant is an evergreen, and is very ornamental.

PRICES: Each   10
15 to 18 in., very strong $0.75 $6.00
12 to 15 in., strong................... .50   4.00

Eriobotrya Japonica.

Loquat: Japan Medlar; Biwa of the Japanese.

This plant is well adapted to the south coastal belt. Trees of medium height, with long, glossy, evergreen leaves; fruit. bright yellow, round or oblong, about the size of a Wild Goose Plum; borne in clusters from end of February until May; seldom perfects fruit in this locality, but is very successful southward.

Eriobotrya; Seedlings.   Each   10   100
4-yr. plants, open ground $0.50 $4.00
3-yr. plants, from pots .... .35   3.00 $25.00
2-yr. plants, from pots .... .25   2.00   17.50

Eriobotrya, Giant. Fruit four times as large as the common Japanese Medlar seedling; very handsome foliage.

PRICES: Each   10
Strong, 2-yr., grafted plants $0.50 $4.00

Mulberries

PRICES, except where noted: Each   10   100
2-year, grafted, very heavy, branched, 8 to 10 ft. $0.50 $4.00 $30.00
1-year, grafted. 7 to 9 ft., heavy .35   3.00   25.00
1-year, grafted, 5 to 7 ft. ..... .25   2.00   15.00

Downing. Fruit of rich. subacid flavor; lasts six weeks. Stands winter of western and middle states.

Hicks. Wonderfully prolific; fruit sweet; excellent for poultry and hogs. Fruit produced during four months.

New American. Fruit similar to Downing, but tree hardier, strong growth, very productive. Bears through a period of two months.

Stubbs.—Originated in Laurens County, Georgia. A tree of fine growth, beautiful foliage; fruit is of enormous size, frequently two inches in length, quality excellent; lasts about two months; an extremely rare variety.

PRICES: Each   10   100
2-year, budded $0.50 $4.00 $30.00
1-year, budded .... .25   2.00   17.50

Olives

Picholine. A variety much esteemed for its rapid growth and early bearing. The tree is also less subject to damage by insects than most other varieties, and ripens its fruit in twelve months, thus bearing a crop annually. Makes excellent oil, and stands with the best for pickling. Olives have been cultivated on the coast of Georgia and South Carolina for many years, and an excellent quality of oil has been produced. A peculiarity of the Olive is that it flourishes and bears abundant crops on rocky and barren soils. where no other fruit trees are successful.

PRICES: Each   10   100
18 to 24 in., branched, from pots and open ground.......$0.35 $3.00 $25.00
15 to 18 in., from pots and open ground .... .25   2.00   17.50

Pomegranates

The Pomegranate is hardy in the gulf states and central sections of Georgia and the Carolinas. The plants will frequently attain a height of upward of 20 feet. It is of good form and foliage; bright scarlet flowers make it a most ornamental plant. It bears early and profusely. The demand for the fruit is increasing in eastern markets, and the Pomegranate is being grown in some sections on an extensive scale. The fruit carries well to distant markets.

PRICES: Each   10   100
3 to 3½ ft., very bushy $0.50   4.00
2 to 3 ft., bushy .... .25   2.25 $20.00

Paper Shell. A new variety from California. Extra fine quality. Will bear first year after transplanting. Skin very thin; hence the name Paper Shell.

Purple-Seeded. Spanish Ruby. Large; yellow, with crimson cheek; flesh purplish crimson, sweet; best quality.

Rhoda. Large, thin skin; sweet; of good flavor.

Subacid. Very large; highly colored. Pulp juicy, subacid.

Sweet. Fruit very large; brilliantly colored.

Hydrangea Monstrosa

P. J. BERCKMANS CO.

Ornamental Department

Deciduous Shrubs

It is seldom that a home in the country, suburbs or town cannot be improved in appearance and greatly enhanced in value by the judicious treatment of the grounds, irrespective of size; and for this purpose many flowering shrubs lend themselves most admirably. Shrubbery, properly planted and massed, is most effective in bringing out certain features of the lawn, to screen some unsightly building or object, or to break the outline of foundation walls.

Along the drive, the walk or the edge of the lawn, borders of shrubs may be planted that will give a succession of bloom from early spring until frost. Even after the leaves have dropped, the brilliant berries and branches of many varieties add cheer and color to the winter landscape. Frequently one finds a spot that suggests the use of an individual specimen—in such case a variety should be selected that will develop symmetrically.

The demand for ornamental shrubs increases annually, and to meet this we have increased our plantings; and our acreage in ornamentals is larger than ever before, and we are in a position to supply many varieties in carload lots. In addition to the shrubs that are best adapted to the various sections of the South we grow many of the hardier kinds suited to the colder sections of the North and North-West.

PLANTING AND CULTIVATING SHRUBS.

The same directions for the preparation of the soil and planting as given for deciduous fruit trees on page 4 apply to the average deciduous shrub. We cannot, however, too strongly emphasize the necessity of keeping the ground free from weeds and grass, and loose by frequent stirring, after being planted.

Do not fail to properly prune your shrubs as soon as planted. The success of your plants depends upon proper pruning. All deciduous shrubs should be pruned annually. The tops and branches should be cut back one-third or one-half if necessary; all dead branches and weak growths should be removed, and care must be exercised not to cut off the blooming wood. All shrubs that flower on the previous year's growth should not be pruned until June or July, or after the blooming period has passed. To this class belong the Altheas, Cydonias, Deutzias, Forsythias, Philadelphus, Spiræas, etc., but such varieties as Ceanothus, Hydrangea, Lonicera, Lilac, etc., which produce flowers upon the young growth, should be pruned during winter. Do not fail to fertilize your shrubs at least once a year.

PRICES OF SPECIAL COLLECTIONS:

We will supply 10 shrubs in 10 varieties, standard size, our selection, for .... $ 1.50
Or 100 shrubs in 25 or 50 varieties, standard size, our selection, for 10.00
Or 10 shrubs in 10 varieties, extra heavy, our selection, for 2.00
Or 100 shrubs in 25 or 50 varieties, extra heavy, our selection, for 15.00

Acacia

Acacia Farnesiana (*Popinac*). A well-known and popular plant; branches thorny; foliage with minute leaflets; flowers in round, yellow balls; very fragrant. Used in Southern France for perfumery. Blooms freely in February and March. Hardy at Savannah and southward.

	Each	10
24 to 30 in., from 4-in. pots	$0.50	$4.00

Althea frutex

Hibiscus Syriacus: **Rose of Sharon**

The flowers are produced from May until September. When planted in masses of contrasting colors, the effect is most pleasing. The varieties we offer are nearly all of dwarf growth and are far superior to the old sorts.

PRICES, except where noted: Each 10 100
Extra strong, well-branched, grafted, 4 to 5 feet $0.50 $4.00 $30.00
Well branched, grafted, 3 to 4 feet .... .40 3.00 25.00
Strong, grafted, branched, 2 to 3 feet .... .25 2.00 15.00

Althæa amplissima. Double; deep rosy-pink, with carmine center; medium grower; early bloomer.

A. coelestis. Single; deep violet-blue, with darker center. A magnificent and distinct variety. Early and continuous bloomer. Dwarf. One of the best.

PRICES: Each 10 100
Well branched, grafted, 2 to 3 feet $0.40 $3.00 $25.00
18 to 24 in., grafted, branched.. .25 2.00 15.00

A. Comte de Hainault. Semi-double; pale pink, shading to a crimson center; medium grower; fine variety; late bloomer.

A. double pink. Originated by us. Double pink, tinged lilac, crimson center; late bloomer; dwarf.

A. Duchess de Brabant. Double dark red; medium grower; late bloomer.

A. Granville. Semi-double; flesh with crimson center. Medium grower; early bloomer.

A. Jeanne d'Arc. The best double, pure white Althæa yet introduced. A tall grower; late bloomer.

A. Lady Stanley. Double; blush-white, with crimson center; medium grower; early bloomer.

A. Louis II. Semi-double; flesh with carmine center. Tall grower; late bloomer.

A. Meehanii (*Variegated-leaved Althaea*). Robust habit compact and somewhat dwarf. Leaves variegated; creamy white, with irregular margins and green centers; never sun-scalds. Flowers single, 3½ to 4 inches in diameter—of a satiny lavender sheen, and purple blotched at the base of each of the five petals; blooms from June until autumn. This variety must not be confused with Buistii, or A. variegata, whose double wine-colored flowers never open and remain unsightly.

PRICES: Each 10
18 to 24 in., grafted, bushy $0.40 $3.00
12 to 18 in., grafted, branched....... .25 2.00

A. Monstrosa. Semi-double; white, crimson center; tall grower.

A. puniceous roseus. Single; rosy-lilac, crimson center; large flowers; profuse bloomer; very handsome.

A. purpurea semi-plena. Originated by us. Flowers large, semi-double, violet-purple, crimson center; free bloomer; tall.

A. rubra pleno. Double; rosy red, with crimson center; medium grower; very fine; late bloomer.

A. Totus albus. Single; pure white; profuse bloomer. Very fine; dwarf grower; late bloomer.

PRICES: Each 10 100
2 to 3 ft., grafted, branched .. $0.40 $3.00
18 to 24 in., grafted, branched .25 2.00 $15.00

A. violacea semi-plena. Semi-double; deep purple-magenta, with crimson center; tall grower; late bloomer.

A. Violet Claire. Clear violet; crimson center; semi-double. Tall grower; late bloomer.

AUGUSTA, GEORGIA.

Azalea

Azalea calendulacea (*A. lutea*). GREAT FLAME Azalea. This is one of our most magnificent native flowering shrubs, producing, about the middle of April, quantities of clusters of large flowers of many shades of yellow, orange, buff, and shades of red. The plant remains in bloom for several weeks. Some plants attain a height of from 6 to 8 feet. When planted in masses, its great beauty is brought out.

PRICES: Each 10
2-2½ ft., strong clumps $1.75 $15.00
18-24 in., clumps 1.25 10.00
18-24 in., well branched .... .75 6.00
12-18 in., well branched .... .50 4.00

A. Nudiflorum. PINXTER FLOWER; WOOD HONEYSUCKLE. The well-known native variety which produces pinkish-white flowers in early April before the leaves appear.

PRICES: Each 10
3-4 ft., heavy clumps $2.00 $15.00
2-3 ft., heavy bushes .... .75 6.00
18-24 in., well branched .... .50 4.00

Berberis. Berberry.

Berberis Vulgaris Atro-purpurea. PURPLE-LEAVED BARBERRY. A form of the European Barberry, but with bright foliage; small, bright yellow flowers, borne in great profusion last of April; a most conspicuous plant; very effective when properly planted with other shrubs. This plant usually attains a height of 5 to 6 feet.

PRICES: Each 10 100
3-4 ft., very bushy $0.50 $4.00 $30.00
2-3 ft., very bushy .... .35 2.50 20.00
18-24 in., well branched ..... .25 2.00 15.00

B. Thunbergii. THUNBERG'S BARBERRY. A dwarf and graceful shrub from Japan. Leaves small, bright green, changing in autumn to beautiful shades of orange, scarlet and crimson; berries red, produced in great profusion, and lasting throughout the winter. Makes a beautiful hedge.

30 to 36 in., very bushy $0.75 $6.00
24 to 30 in., very bushy...... .50 4.00 $30.00
12 to 18 in., well branched.... .25 2.00 15.00

Buddleia

PRICES: Each 10 100
4-5 ft., very bushy $0.50 $4.00 $30.00
3-4 ft., well branched......... .30 2.50 20.00

Buddleia officinalis. A new variety from China with pale-green leaves, silvery beneath. Plant attains a height from 6 to 10 ft.; small, violet-colored flowers are produced in January on racemes 6 to 10 inches long. The plant continue to bloom for several weeks, but owing to its early blooming is recommended only for Savannah and southward.

B. Variabilis Magnifica. BUTTERFLY BUSH. Similar to Buddleia Variabilis Veitchiana, but flowers of a deeper shade of violet; plant is also a taller grower; blooms from June until frost; very fragrant. The best Buddleia yet introduced.

B. Variabilis Veitchiana. Another beautiful new shrub from China with very dark-green leaves; plant attains a height of from 6 to 8 feet; flowers violet with orange throat, borne in arching racemes 12 to 15 inches in length; commences to bloom in June and lasts until frost; very fragrant; a most desirable plant.

Callicarpa. French Mulberry.

PRICES: Each 10
4 to 5 ft., heavy, well branched........$0.50 $4.00
3 to 4 ft., well branched .... .35 3.00
2 to 3 ft., branched.................. .25 2.00

Callicarpa Americana. FRENCH MULBERRY. With purple berries, produced in clusters; very effective in fall and early winter. This beautiful native plant is not sufficiently appreciated.

C. Americana alba. A form of French Mulberry, with white berries. A very distinct and rare plant. Introduced by us. In late fall and early winter the plant is covered with a mass of snow-white berries, making it a very conspicuous object.

Calycanthus. Sweet Shrub.

Calycanthus floridus. (*Butneria florida*). SWEET, OR STRAWBERRY SHRUB. Our native sweet or brown shrub. Flowers double. Chocolate-colored; very fragrant. Blooms in April.

PRICES: Each 10
2 to 3 ft., well branched...............$0.25 $2.00

C. Glaucus. (*C. loevigatus*; *Butneria fertilis*). CAROLINA ALLSPICE OR SWEET SHRUB. A more vigorous grower and a more profuse bloomer than C. Floridus. The very fragrant, chocolate-colored flowers are also larger; attains a height of from 6 to 8 ft.; blooms in April.

PRICES: Each 10
2 to 3 ft. $0.25 $2.00

C. Praecox. (*Chimonanthus fragrans*). ORIENTAL SWEET SHRUB. A Japanese shrub, producing exquisitely fragrant yellow flowers, usually about January 1st, and lasting for about four weeks. The flowers appear before the leaves, and when in full bloom it is a most pleasing plant. It blooms at a period when our gardens are scarce of flowers.

PRICES: Each 10 100
4 to 5 ft., very bushy $1.00 $8.00
3 to 4 ft., very bushy .... .75 5.00 $35.00
2 to 3 ft., well branched ...... .50 3.00
18 to 24 in., branched .... .25 2.00 15.00

Caryopteris. Blue Spiraea.

Caryopteris Mastacanthus. BLUE SPIRAEA OR CHINESE BEARDWORT. A free-blooming, dwarf-growing shrub; flowers lavender-blue produced in great profusion in early summer and lasts until autumn. Very effective for massing. In the colder sections this plant is treated as herbaceous.

PRICES: Each 10 100
24-30 inches, very bushy, field-grown, ...$0.50 $4.00 $30.00
18-24 inches, bushy, field-grown .25 2.00 17.50

Cassia

Cassia Florabunda. A free-flowering plant; perfectly hardy here. Large, orange-yellow, pea-shaped flowers, produced in great profusion from July until frost. Attains a height of 6 to 8 feet. A most effective lawn plant.

PRICES: Each 10 100
Strong, bushy, 4-5 ft........$0.50 $4.00 $30.00
Strong, 3-4 ft. .... .25 2.00 17.50

Ceanothus. New Jersey Tea.

Ceanothus. Marie Simon. A bautiful shrub of medium growth, producing, in early April, a great profusion of small purple-lilac flowers which last for several weeks. A very desirable plant of easy cultivation. In this section it is almost an evergreen.

PRICES: Each 10
3 years, very bushy $0.50 $4.00
2 years, bushy .... .35 3.00

Cercis. Judas Tree.

Cercis Japonica. (*Cercis Chinenses*). JAPAN JUDAS TREE. Leaves heart-shaped, deep, shining green, assuming a yellow color in autumn. Rosy pink flowers, with a purple cast. Blooms in March.

PRICES: Each 10
6-7 ft., very bushy $2.00 $15.00
5-6 ft., very bushy 1.50 12.50
4 to 5 ft., bushy 1.00 8.00
3 to 4 ft., bushy .... .75 6.50
2-3 ft., well branched .... .50 4.00

C. Siliquastrum. A new form which originated in our Nursery. A large growing shrub or small tree; leaves heart-shaped, and, like the other Cercis, assumes a yellow tone in autumn. This Judas Tree is the most profuse bloomer we have ever seen; deep lavender colored flowers, four times as large as that of our native Judas Tree. They are produced in large bunches, and when in full bloom, the tree is

23

P. J. BERCKMANS CO.

CERCIS—Continued.

an entire mass of color. We have tested this variety for several years, and, in offering it, we are sure that it will become a great favorite. The original plant is about 12 ft. in height.

PRICES: Each   10
3-4 ft., well branched, budded.........$1.00
2-3 ft., well branched, budded.......... .75 $6.00

Chilopsis.

PRICES: Each   10
4 years, very bushy, 6-8 ft............$0.75 $6.00
3 years, very bushy.................... .50   4.00
2 years, heavy......................... .25   2.00

Chilopsis linearis. FLOWERING WILLOW. A tall-growing shrub or small tree from southwest Texas; leaves linear; flowers lilac striped with yellow; lobes beautifully crimped; blooms continuously from April until frost. Does well in dry situations.

C. Linearis alba.. Similar to Linearis, but with pure white blooms; a fine variety.

Chionanthus

Chionanthus Virginica. WHITE FRINGE. A very ornamental native shrub. In early April the plant is literally covered with white, fringe-like flowers.

PRICES: Each   10
3-4 ft., large bushes $0.75
2-3 ft., large bushes .... .50 $4.00
18-24 in., well branched............... .35   3.00

Citrus.

Citrus trifoliata. HARDY ORANGE. As an ornamental flowering plant, few are more desirable. The plant attains a height of 10 to 15 feet, and is very bushy and thorny; foliage trifoliate, retained quite late, but is not an evergreen here; however, the vivid green wood gives it an evergreen appearance during winter. In early March the plant is covered with a mass of large, single, white flowers, and a second and third crop of blooms, of smaller size, are produced during summer. The bright golden fruit is retained during winter, which makes this plant a showy garden feature. It is also an excellent hedge plant.

PRICES: Each   10   100
Extra strong, well branched,
3-4 ft., well branched, 3 yrs..$0.25 $2.00 $15.00

For smaller sizes, see under Hedge Plants, page 51.

Corchorus.   Kerria.

Corchorus Japonica fl. pl. GLOBE FLOWER; JAPANESE ROSE. A desirable shrub of spreading habit with double yellow flowers about an inch in diameter. Effective for massing, attains a height of about 6 to 8 feet. Blooms continuously from early April until frost.

Original Plant of Citrus trifoliata at Fruitlands.

PRICES: Each   10   100
3 to 4 ft., heavy clumps........$0.50 $4.00
2 to 3 ft., well branched........ .25   2.00 $17.50

Cornus.   Osier Dogwood.

Cornus sanguinea. EUROPEAN RED OSIER. A shrub of spreading habit; purplish red branches; flowers greenish white, in compact clusters, which are produced last of April, followed by black berries; attains a height of 8 to 10 feet. Desirable for massing.

PRICES: Each   10   100
4-5 ft., very bushy $0.50 $4.00 $30.00
3-4 ft., heavy, well branched.. .35   3.00   20.00
2-3 ft., well branched......... .25   2.00   15.00

Sibirica. (C. Alba). RED SIBERIAN OSIER. An upright shrub with bright red branches, which are most conspicuous in winter; flowers creamy white in numerous small panicles; fruit light blue. This shrub usually attains a height of 6 to 10 feet.

PRICES: Each   10   100
3-4 ft., very bushy............$0.50 $4.00 $30.00
2-3 ft., heavy, well branched.... .35   3.00   20.00
18-24 in., well branched....... .25   2.00

CRAPE MYRTLE. See Lagerstroemia

Cydonia.   Pyrus.

Cydonia Japonica. JAPAN QUINCE, OR FIRE BUSH. Flowers vary from dark red to lighter shades of red, salmon and pink. Have also a pure white variety.

PRICES: Each   10   100
3 to 4 ft., heavy, well
branched $0.35 $3.00
2 to 3 ft., well branched .... .25   2.00 $15.00

Deutzia

PRICES, except where noted.
                             Each   10   100
5 to 6 ft., extra heavy $0.60 $5.00 $30.00
4 to 5 ft., very heavy .... .40   3.00   20.00
3 to 4 ft., heavy .... .30   2.50   17.50
2 to 3 ft., well branched.......... .25   2.00   15.00

Deutzia crenata. SINGLE WHITE DEUTZIA. Flowers pure white, single, produced in great profusion in April. A tall grower.

D. crenata flore plena alba. D. candidissima. Flowers pure white, double, produced in great abundance middle of April. A tall-growing variety.

D. crenata flore plena rosea. DOUBLE PINK DEUTZIA. Same as Deutzia crenata flore plena alba, except that some of the outer petals are rosy purple. Very desirable; blooms last of April, or a little later than Pride of Rochester.

D. gracilis. Flowers pure white, bell-shaped; quite dwarf; is also valuable as a pot-plant for winter blooming in conservatory. Blooms early in April.

PRICES: Each   10   100
2-2½ ft., heavy clumps $0.50 $4.00
18-24 in., very bushy .... .35   3.00 $20.00
12-18 in., well branched ..... .25   2.00   17.50

D. Lemoinei. Flowers pure white; borne in great profusion on stout, upright branches; dwarf habit. A most desirable and satisfactory variety. Blooms early in April.

PRICES: Each   10   100
2 to 3 ft., very bushy $0.35 $3.00 $20.00
18 to 24 in., bushy .... .25   2.00   17.50

D. Pride of Rochester. Double white, back of petals faintly tinted with pink; large panicles; blooms middle of April, and continues to bloom three or four weeks.

DOGWOOD. See Cornus

Elaeagnus   Japanese Oleaster.

Elaeagnus edulis (Longipes). Gumi fruit of the Japanese. A low-growing ornamental shrub. In early April produces very fragrant, reddish-yellow flowers which are immediately followed by bright red edible fruit, which is one-third of an inch in length; oblong, covered with minute white dots. This fruit will

AUGUSTA, GEORGIA.

Hibiscus aurantiaca. Large, double, salmon-colored flowers, with carmine center.
H. cruentus. Double; clear carmine. Free bloomer.
H. Lambertii. Vivid red; single.
H. miniatus. Vivid red; double.
H. Peachblow. A beautiful shade of pink; double.
H. sub-violaceus. Crimson-violet; semi-double.
H. grandiflora. Very large, single, red flowers.

HONEYSUCKLE. See Lonicera

Hydrangea

When given a rich, moist soil, where they are protected from the afternoon sun of summer, and the plants kept well enriched, there is nothing more attractive than a mass of well-developed specimen Hydrangeas. They are also very desirable when grown singly or in tubs. Several varieties, such as Monstrosa, Otaksa and Rosea, vary in color from pale rose to blue. This variation is due to certain chemicals contained in the soil.

PRICES, except where noted:

	Each	10	100
3 yrs., heavy, well branched, 24 to 30 inches	$0.50	$4.00	$30.00
2 yrs., strong, well branched, 18 to 24 inches	.35	3.00	25.00
Branched, 12 to 18 inches	.25	2.00	18.00

Hydrangea arborescens grandiflora. A recent introduction of great value. Blooms very large, snowy white. A valuable acquisition, as it begins to bloom in April and lasts almost the entire summer. In form the panicles are similar to H. hortensis.

PRICES:

	Each	10
2-3 ft., extra heavy	$0.50	$4.00
18-24 in., heavy	.35	3.00

Hydrangea Avalanche. Large corymbs of pure white flowers. A splendid improvement on all other white sorts.

H. La Lorraine. (New). Very large flowers; pale rose, turning to bright pink; sometimes blue.
H. monstrosa. A very large-flowering variety; beautiful rose color, shaded white; in some soils pale rose or blue. A very decided improvement on Otaksa.
H. Otaksa. An improved variety of Hortensis; flowerheads very large; pale rose or blue, according to soil.
H. paniculata grandiflora. Produces in July immense panicles of pure white flowers, which last for several weeks; a most valuable shrub. A large bed of this plant makes a most striking appearance. This shrub

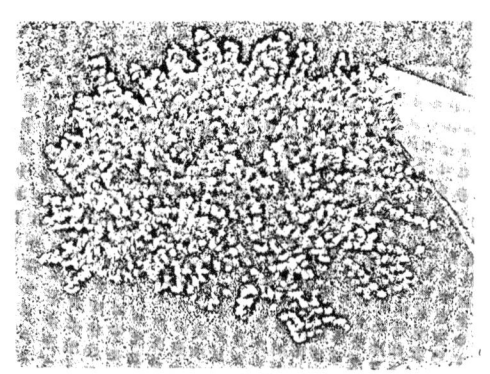

Deutzia Lemoinei.

ELAEAGNUS—Continued.

make an excellent jelly and marmalade; flavor is sharp, pungent, and rather agreeable; foliage light green, silvery-beneath. A beautiful ornamental shrub, almost evergreen.

PRICES:

	Each	10	100
2 to 3 ft., strong, bushy	$0.50	$4.00	
18 to 24 inches, bushy	.35	3.00	$25.00
12 to 18 inches, strong, well branched	.25	2.00	17.50

Exochorda. Pearl Bush.

Exochorda grandiflora (*Spiraea grandiflora*). A desirable, large,growing shrub, attains a height of from 8 to 10 ft. Large, pure white flowers produced in great profusion about middle of March. When in full bloom the plant has the appearance of a snow bank. When planted in a mass this plant is most conspicuous.

PRICES:

	Each	10	100
4 to 5 ft., extra heavy	$0.60	$5.00	$35.00
3 to 4 ft., very heavy	.50	4.00	25.00
2 to 3 ft., heavy	.35	3.00	20.00
18 to 24 in., well branched	.25	2.00	15.00

Forsythia. Golden Bell.

PRICES:

	Each	10	100
3 yrs., 3-4 ft., well branched	$0.35	$3.00	
2 yrs., 2-3 ft., well branched	.25	2.00	$15.00

Forsythia Fortunei, FORTUNE'S GOLDEN BELL. Similar to F. Suspensa, but habit is more upright and vigorous. Flowers golden-yellow, frequently with twisted petals. A desirable variety. Grows to a height of 8 to 10 feet. Blooms in March.

F. intermedia, HYBRID GOLDEN BELL. A tall variety with slender, arching branches; flowers golden-yellow, produced in great profusion. Attains a height of from 8 to 10 ft.; blooms in March.

F. suspensa, DROOPING GOLDEN BELL. A graceful variety with long, slender, drooping branches. Leaves dark, shining green; flowers yellow, produced in great profusion in March. Attains a height of 6 to 10 feet.

F. viridissima, GOLDEN BELL. Flowers golden yellow, produced in great profusion last of February or early in March. Most effective when planted in large groups.

FRENCH MULBERRY. See Callicarpa
GLOBE FLOWER. See Corchorus

Hibiscus rosa Sinensis

Perfectly hardy in South Florida. Blooms continuously.

PRICES:

	Each	10	100
Very strong plants, from 3½ and 4-inch pots	$0.50	$4.00	$30.00
Strong plants, from 3-in. pots	.25	2.00	15.00

Hypericum Moserianum.

P. J. BERCKMANS CO.

HYDRANGEA—Continued.

should be grown in rich ground and cut back severely during winter. It will then produce magnificent flower-heads.

PRICES:
	Each	10	100
3 to 4 feet, well branched	$0.50	$4.00	$30.00
2 to 3 feet, well branched	.35	3.00	25.00
18 to 24 inches, well branched	.25	2.00	18.00

H. ramis pictis, or Red-branched. With dark purple stems and large heads of rose or pale blue flowers, with lighter center. Blooms in early May.

H. rosea. Vigorous habit. Flower-heads shaped like those of Thomas Hogg; freely produced. Color bright, rosy pink. Blooms in early May.

H. Souv. de Claire. Somewhat similar to Otaksa, but with smaller heads of bloom, which are produced in great profusion. Bright pink.

H. Thomas Hogg. One of the best white-flowered variety of the Hortensis group. Flowers last several weeks. At first slightly tinted green, becoming pure white. Blooms in early May.

Hydrangea, Standard or Tree Form

Hydrangea paniculata grandiflora. These plants have been trained to a single stem, and have large, bushy heads. Conspicuous as single specimens on the lawn.

PRICES:
	Each	10
4 to 5 feet	$1.00	$8.00
3 to 4 feet	.75	6.00

Hypericum

Hypericum Moserianum. GOLDEN ST. JOHN'S WORT. A beautiful dwarf shrub, attaining a height of one to two feet. In this section almost an evergreen; leaves dark-green; large, single, bright, golden-yellow flowers two inches in diameter produced freely during the entire summer; a very desirable plant; most effective when planted in masses. Blooms from early May throughout the entire summer.

PRICES:
	Each	10	100
3 years, very heavy	$0.35	$3.00	
2 years, well-branched	.25	2.00	$17.50

Jasminum. Jasmine.

Jasminum nudiflorum. NAKED-FLOWERED JASMINE. A very graceful, hardy, drooping shrub with dark-green bark which gives the plant the appearance of being evergreen; leaves dark-green; bright yellow flowers freely produced in early January and continuing for some time. One of the finest plants to bloom. Hardy at New York.

	Each	10	100
2-3 ft., very heavy	$0.35	$2.50	$17.50
18-24 in., well-branched	.25	2.00	15.00

J. Revolutum. J. HUMILE; J. FLAVUM; J. TRIUMPHANS. Common Italian Yellow Jasmine; almost evergreen; hardy as far north as Maryland; leaves dark green; bright yellow flowers, produced in April, in open clusters; blooms almost continuously until fall.

PRICES:
	Each	10
4-yrs., very heavy, well-branched	$0.75	$6.00
3-yrs., heavy, branched	.50	4.00
2-yrs., heavy, branched	.25	2.25

Crape Myrtle. Tree Form.

Lagerstroemia. Crape Myrtle.

Lagerstroemia Indica. CRAPE MYRTLE. A very popular and free-flowering shrub, or small tree, which produces blooms in great abundance throughout the summer. The flowers are beautifully fringed and are borne in large clumps. A massing of these, or a single specimen, makes a most striking effect. Commences to bloom in May. We offer three colors—White, Crimson and Pink.

	Each	10	100
5-6 feet, well branched	$1.00	$8.00	
4-5 feet, well branched	.75	6.00	
3-4 feet, well branched	.50	4.00	$30.00
2-3 feet, well branched	.35	3.00	25.00
18-24 in., strong	.25	2.00	18.00

Lagerstroemia. Crape Myrtle.
Tree Form.

We offer a limited quantity of Crimson Crape Myrtle in tree form; 7 to 9 feet high, trunks from 3 to 3½ feet; well formed heads. $2.00 each.

Lonicera. Bush or Upright Honeysuckle.

These plants are vigorous growers and free bloomers, and are readily cultivated.

Prices except where noted
	Each	10	100
3 to 4 feet bushy	$0.35	$3.00	
2 to 3 feet bushy	.25	2.00	$15.00

Lonicera Belgica. BELGIAN, DUTCH, OR MONTHLY FRAGRANT HONEYSUCKLE. Of semi-climbing habit, but can easily be grown in bush form. Pink flowers; very profuse bloomer in early spring. In late summer again produces flowers, which continue until frost. One of our finest shrubs.

PRICES:
	Each	10
2 to 3 feet, heavy	$0.35	$3.00
18 to 24 inches, well branched	.25	2.00

Jasminum nudiflorum.

AUGUSTA, GEORGIA.

LONICERA—Continued.

L. Bella. Hybrid variety; abundance of pinkish white flowers in early spring, followed by yellow fruit.

L. Dr. Bertrance. A new variety, producing an abundance of large pink flowers in early spring, which contrast beautifully with the bright green foliage. A most desirable variety.

L. Fragrantissima. CHINESE FRAGRANT UPRIGHT HONEYSUCKLE. Very strong growing variety; very fragrant, small white flowers appear in early spring before the leaves; foliage is retained until late winter; sometimes in sheltered positions all winter.

L. Grandiflora Rosea. A variety of medium growth; fine foliage, producing in early April beautiful pink flowers; a very distinct variety.

L. Morrowi. JAPANESE BUSH HONEYSUCKLE. A Japanese variety, producing early in April a profusion of white flowers, followed by a mass of bright red fruit.

L. Ruprechtiana. MANCHURIAN HONEYSUCKLE. Flowers pure white. Blooms in March and lasts six weeks; berries red or yellow. A very showy variety.

L. Tartarica. TARTARIAN HONEYSUCKLE. A large-growing variety with dark-green foliage, and pink colored flowers in April, followed by crimson fruit.

PEARL BUSH. See Exochorda.

Philadelphus. Syringa or Mock Orange.

Very handsome vigorous growing shrubs with large foliage and beautiful flowers, which are produced in great profusion the latter part of April and early May.

PRICES: Except where noted. Each 10 100
5 to 6 feet extra heavy $0.60 $5.00 $35.00
4 to 5 feet very heavy .... .50 4.00 25.00
3 to 4 feet very heavy .... .35 3.00 20.00
2 to 3 feet well-branched ..... .25 2.00 15.00

Philadelphus Avalanche. Very graceful, with slender, arching branches, which are almost entirely covered with white, sweet-scented, showy flowers; dwarf, compact habit.
Each 10
2 to 3 feet heavy $0.35 $3.00
18 to 24 inch heavy .... .25 2.00

P. Bouquet Blanc. A fine new variety with semi-double white flowers; very free bloomer.
Each 10
2 to 3 feet, heavy...................$0.35 3.00
18 to 24 inch heavy .... .25 2.00

P. Conquette. A very desirable new variety with large, sweet-scented flowers; dwarf grower.
Each 10
2 to 3 feet $0.35 $3.00
18 to 24 inches .... .25 2.00

P. Coronarius. GARLAND OR SWEET SYRINGA. Flowers pure white, very sweet, produced in great profusion.

P. Gordonianus. GORDON'S MOCK ORANGE. A variety attaining a height from 10 to 12 feet. leaves broad, bright-green; pure white flowers produced in dense racemes; blooms late.

P. Grandiflorus. A conspicuous variety, with very large white flowers.

P. Laxus. Very large white flowers produced in clusters in May, after all other varieties of Philadelphus have finished blooming; foliage very large and distinct. This is a very fine and desirable variety.

P. Lemoinei grandiflora fl. pl. HYBRID MOCK ORANGE. A desirable new variety, with small, bright-green leaves, 1 to 2 inches in length; very fragrant, semi-double white flowers are borne in dense clusters which cover the entire plant. A dwarf grower. Most effective in masses.
Each 10 100
18-24 in. very bushy $0.25 $2.00 $15.00

P. Souv de Billard. Leaves broad, beautiful flowers, late bloomer.

Prunus. Plums.

Double-Flowering Almonds and Plums.
PRICES, EXCEPT WHERE NOTED. Each 10
2 to 3 feet, well-branched, budded......$0.50 $4.00
18 to 24 inches, branched, budded......... .35 3.00
Prunus Japonica flore pleona Alba. (*Amygdalus Pumila*). DWARF DOUBLE WHITE ALMOND. A beautiful dwarf shrub, producing in early spring, before the leaves appear, a mass of small double white flowers. One of the best of the early flowering shrubs.
P. Japonica flore ploena rubra. (*Amygdalus Pumila*). DWARF DOUBLE PINK FLOWERING ALMONDS. Same as the double white Almond, except the flowers are double rose. A very beautiful shrub.
P. triloba. DOUBLE FLOWERING PLUM. A native of China; a very desirable, early-flowering ornamental shrub. Double flowers of a delicate pink shade are produced in enormous quantity along the slender branches. Blooms April 1st.
Each 10
3-4 feet ....$ .50 $4.00
2-3 feet .... .35 3.00

Punica. Pomegranate.

Very valuable, summer-flowering, tall-growing shrubs. Perfectly hardy in the South. Flowers are produced in great profusion very early in May, and last almost during the entire summer. Foliage bright, lustrous green. Very conspicuous and desirable.
Each 10 100
4 to 5 feet, extra heavy, well-
branched $0.75 $6.00
3 to 4 feet, very heavy, well
branched .... .50 4.00 $30.00
2 to 3 feet, branched .... .25 2.00 15.00
Punica granatum alba. Double; white.
P. granatum rubra. Beautiful, double-red flowers are in great profusion very early in May and last almost during the entire summer; a very showy plant.
P. granatum variegatum. Sometimes double-red and double-variegated blooms will appear on the same plant.

PYRUS JAPONICA. See Cydonia.

Rhodotypus. Kerria.

Rhodotypus kerrioides. WHITE KERRIA. A beautiful and distinct Japanese shrub, attaining a height from 4 to 6 feet; large leaves; white flowers an inch or more in diameter freely produced middle of April, followed by black berries which are retained during the winter.
Each 10 100
3 to 4 feet, very bushy.......$0.40 $3.50
2 to 3 feet, bushy............ .35 3.00 $20.00
18 to 24 inches. well-branched.. .25 2.00 17.50

Rhus. Sumac.

Rhus copallina. UPLAND SUMAC. A small tree or large shrub. Leaves are dark green and lustrous, turning ruddy brown in fall. Fruit bright red and persists throughout winter.
Each 10 100
4 to 5 feet $0.35 $3.00 $20.00
3 to 4 feet .... .25 2.00 17.50
R. cotinus. PURPLE FRINGE, OR SMOKE TREE. Greatly admired for its cloud-like masses of very delicate flowers, which appear the last of April and cover the entire plant during the summer. From a distance the plant appears like a cloud of smoke.
Each 10 100
6 to 8 ft., well branched......$1.00 $7.50
5 to 6 ft., well branched...... .75 6.00
4 to 5 ft., branched.......... .50 4.00
3 to 4 ft., branched.......... .25 2.00 $15.00
R. glabra. SMOOTH SUMAC. A shrub or low tree with an open crown. Leaves dark above and white beneath, turning brilliant scarlet in autumn; desirable for massing; flowers in large terminal panicles in May, followed by crimson fruited clusters, which persist all winter.
Each 10 100
6-8 feet, heavy...............$0.50 $4.00 $30.00
5-6 feet, heavy.............. .35 3.00 20.00
4-5 feet .... .25 2.00 17.50

27

P. J. BERCKMANS CO.

Robinia. Locust.

Robina hispida rosea. ROSE OR MOSS LOCUST A native dwarf shrub, usually 2 to 3 feet high; very showy, rose-colored flowers produced in racemes during April. A very attractive and showy plant.

	Each	10
4 to 5 feet, very heavy	$0.75	$6.00
3 to 4 feet, well-branched	.50	4.00
2 to 3 feet, branched	.25	2.25

Rosmarinus. Rosemary.

Rosemarinus Officinalis. A shrubby evergeen with bright blue flowers borne in the axiles of the leaves; one of the old favorites among aromatic shrubs. Very effective in a border or for planting in clumps. Will be cut back to 6 inches to facilitate transplanting.

	Each	10	100
18-24 inches, heavy clumps	$0.50	$4.00	
18-24 inches, very bushy	.35	3.00	$25.00
12-18 inches, bushy	.25	2.00	15.00

Salvia.

Salvia Greggi. HARDY EVER-BLOOMING SALVIA. This is native of Western Texas, and is, therefore, extremely hardy; it can stand zero weather and resists drought. It begins to bloom in early spring and lasts until the blooms are killed by frost, in the fall; the flower is crimson; plant grows to a height of 3 to 4 feet and a corresponding width; very effective for massing; a most satisfactory plant.

	Each	10
Strong, field-grown, three years	$0.50	$4.00
Strong, field-grown, two years	.25	2.25

Spiraea.

PRICES: Except where noted.

	Each	10	100
4-5 feet, extra heavy, bushy	$0.50	$4.00	$30.00
3-4 feet, very heavy, well-branched	.35	3.00	20.00
2-3 feet, well-branched	.25	2.00	15.00

SPRING BLOOMING SPIRAEAS.

S. Opulifolia aurea. GOLDEN-LEAVED NINE-BARK. A vigorous-growing variety, with golden tinted leaves and white flowers, which are freely produced last of April; very conspicuous and pleasing when a golden-leaved plant is desired.

S prunifolia flore pleno. BRIDAL WREATH. A beautiful, early-blooming variety, with small, double white flowers. Commences to bloom early in March.

S. Reevesiana. REEVES' SINGLE SPIRAEA. Produces large clusters of single white flowers, covering the entire bush; flowers very free in early spring; blooms just before Spiraea Reevesiana fl. pl.

S. Reevesiana flore pleno. (*S. Cantonensis flore pleno*). With large, round clusters of double white flowers which cover the entire plant. Blooms latter part of March and continues for several weeks.

Spiraea Thunbergii.

S. Thunbergii. COMMON SNOW GARLAND. A beautiful dwarf variety, with many slender branches, forming a dense bush. The leaves in autumn assume brilliant shades of orange and scarlet. Profuse bloomer. Desirable for a low hedge.

	Each	10	100
3-3½ ft., extra heavy specimens	$0.60	$5.00	$40.00
2½-3 ft., extra heavy specimens	.50	4.00	30.00
2-2½ ft., heavy bushes	.35	3.00	20.00
18-24 in., heavy, well-branched	.25	2.00	15.00

S. Van Houttei. VAN HOUTTE'S SPIRAEA. A graceful shrub, growing 6 to 8 feet in height. Produces a profusion of single white flowers during the latter part of March. One of the most popular Spiraeas.

PERPETUAL BLOOMING SPIRAEAS.

Spiraea Anthony Waterer. CRIMSON SPIRAEA. An improvement upon S. Bumaldi. A remarkably free-flowering shrub, with upright branches. Attains a height of about 3 feet. Leaves bright green, with frequent variegations of yellow. If blooms are cut off as soon as they begin to fade, the plant will bloom the entire season. Makes a low-growing hedge.

	Each	10
18-24 inches, very bushy	$0.35	$3.00
12-18 inches, bushy	.25	2.00

S. Billardi. BILLARD'S SPIRAEA. A tall-growing variety. Flowers bright pink, produced in long dense panicles; commences to bloom in May and lasts throughout the summer. Very showy.

S. Callosa alba. FORTUNE'S DWARF WHITE SPIRAEA. Flowers white, of very dwarf growth. Commences to bloom early in April.

	Each	10	100
2 to 2½ ft., extra heavy, bushy	$0.50	$4.00	$30.00
1½ to 2 ft., very bushy	.35	3.00	20.00
12 to 18 inches, very bushy	.25	2.00	

S. Fortunei Macrophylla. A variety with very large leaves, which are tinted royal purple, making the plant very conspicuous. Very effective for a border or for planting in groups.

	Each	10
12 to 18 inches, very bushy	$0.25	$2.00

S. Proebeli. A fine, free-blooming sort; rosy-colored flowers, produced last of April in large, flat heads. The young foliage tinted dark red.

	Each	10	100
18 to 24 inches, very bushy	$0.35	$3.00	$20.00
12 to 18 inches, very bushy	.25	2.00	15.00

Stephanandra

Stephanandra flexuosa. A very graceful and desirable shrub, attaining a height of 3 to 4 ft., with spreading, drooping branches; leaves serrated. At the time of unfolding these are tinted with red. During the summer the leaves are of a deep glossy green, and in autumn tones of reddish-purple are assumed. White flowers in soft feathery racemes are produced in May.

	Each	10	100
2 to 3 ft., bushy	$0.35	$3.00	
18 to 24 inches, bushy	.25	2.00	$17.50

Styrax. Storax.

Styrax Japonica. JAPANESE STORAX. A beautiful Japanese shrub with spreading branches and bright green leaves; fragrant white flowers produced in drooping racemes middle of April. This shrub attains a height of from 8 to 12 ft. It is a most desirable variety, and should be in every collection.

	Each	10
5 to 6 ft., very heavy, well branched	$1.00	$8.00
4 to 5 ft., heavy, well branched	.75	6.00
3 to 4 ft., well branched	.50	4.00
2 to 3 ft., well branched	.35	3.00
18 to 24 inches, well branched	.25	2.00

ST. JOHN'S WORT. See Hypericum.

SWEET SHRUB. See Calycanthus.

Symphoricarpos.

	Each	10	100
2 to 3 ft., well branched,	$0.35	$3.00	
18 to 24 inches, well branched	.25	2.00	$15.00

Symphoricarpos racemosus. SNOWBERRY. A graceful shrub, growing 4 to 6 feet tall; slender, drooping branches; flowers white, followed by clusters of white berries, which remain upon the plant for months.

S. vulgaris. CORAL BERRY. A native shrub, growing naturally from New York to Texas. Purplish red berries are produced in great profusion. They remain upon the plant all winter, making it especially desirable for landscape planting; 4 to 6 feet tall.

Syringa. Lilac.

These old-fashioned shrubs have been popular for ages. Our collection embraces some of the old as well as the cream of the new European sorts. By a judicious selection you can have the blooming period of the Lilac extended over a month. The first blooms appear here the latter part of March. The Lilac will give the best results in fertile soils, moderately moist, but well drained.

PRICES, except where noted. All grafted plants:

	Each	10	100
3 to 4 feet, extra heavy, well branched	$0.60	$4.00	$30.00
2 to 3 ft., heavy, well branched	.50	3.00	20.00
18 to 24 in., branched	.25	2.00	17.50

LILAC, SINGLE VARIETIES

Charles X. Strong grower; trusses large, reddish purple.

Frau Dammann. A fine white, with large panicles of flowers of medium size; an early bloomer.

Gloria Rupella. Dark lilac; extra early; profuse bloomer.

Lovaniensis. Silvery pink; a distinct and beautiful shade; large panicles.

Ludwig Spath. Dark purplish red. Very distinct.

Marie Legraye. Large panicles of single white flowers. One of the finest white Lilacs, and it is greatly used for forcing under glass.

Lilac.

Pekinensis. CHINESE LILAC. This is a very large growing variety, and can almost be termed a tree, as it attains a height of 15 to 20 ft. Large panicles of small, creamy-white flowers are produced in great profusion about the last of April, and continue to bloom for about six weeks.

	Each	10
6 to 7 ft., extra heavy bushes	$1.50	$10.00
5 to 6 ft., extra heavy	1.00	8.00
3 to 4 ft., heavy	.35	

Persica. PERSIAN LILAC. Small foliage, flowers bright purple. A fine old sort.

Persica Laciniata. PERSIAN LILAC. Foliage finely cut; flowers bright purple.

Prof. Stockhardt. Lavender; large trusses; extra early. An extra good sort.

Uncle Tom. Large spikes of single flowers; very dark purple; one of the darkest of all Lilacs.

Vulgaris. COMMON LILAC. Bluish-purple flowers; very fragrant.

LILAC, DOUBLE VARIETIES

Alphonse Lavallee. Blue, shaded violet; large panicles; a good sort.

Charles Joly. Very dark reddish purple; excellent.

Comte de Jessien. Lilac-blue; very fine.

Comte Horace de Choiseul. Porcelain-blue in bud; white when open. Large trusses; profuse bloomer.

Dame Blanc. Beautiful double white flowers; one of the best.

Dr. Masters. Clear lilac; superb.

Emile Lemoine. Rosy lilac; very large and beautiful.

Jeanne d'Arc. Very large spikes, with pure double white flowers; very fine.

La Tour d'Auvergne. Flowers very large; violet-purple. Extra good; a profuse bloomer.

Le Gaulois. Panicles very large and compact; deep peach color.

Louis Henri. Rosy lilac; extra fine; blooms early.

Miss Ellen Willmott. Snow-white double flowers of perfect shape; very fine.

Mme. Casimir Perier. Beautiful white flowers in large and compact panicles. One of the most prolific.

Matthieu de Dombasle. Reddish mauve; buds purplish.

Michael Buchner. Pale lilac; very large panicles.

Pres. Carnot. Pale lilac. A fine, early bloomer.

Pyramidalis. Pale lilac; carmine in bud. An extra fine, profuse bloomer.

Renoncule. Purplish lilac. A free bloomer; extra fine.

Tamarix. Tamarisk.

Tall-growing shrubs, with slender branches and small, delicate leaves which resemble the cypress. Flowers small, pink, produced in great abundance. An excellent plant for the seashore.

PRICES, except where noted.

	Each	10	100
6 to 8 feet, very heavy, well branched	$0.60	$5.00	$40.00
5 to 6 feet, very heavy, well branched	.50	4.00	30.00
4 to 5 feet, well branched	.25	2.00	15.00

Tamarix Gallica. FRENCH TAMARISK. Foliage light glaucous green; flowers pink in summer.

T. hispida aestivalis. The finest of all Tamarisks. Commences to bloom in early May, and if kept in a vigorous condition, continues throughout the entire summer. Foliage bright green; flowers bright carmine-pink; Very scarce.

	Each	10
4 to 5 feet, well branched	$0.50	$4.00
3 to 4 feet, well branched	.25	2.00

T. odessana. CASPIAN TAMARISK. A new variety, with pale rose flowers, blooming earlier than T. Gallica.

T. Plumosa or Japonica. JAPANESE TAMARISK. Of medium height; foliage very graceful and feathery; a beautiful variety; blooms early in April.

P. J. BERCKMANS CO.

Viburnum. Snowball.

Viburnum Lantana. WAYFARING TREE. A large shrub, 10 to 15 feet tall. Flowers white, produced in large cymes in April. Berries bright red, changing to black.

	Each	10
3 to 4 feet, bushy	$0.50	$4.00
2 to 3 feet, well branched	.35	3.00
18 to 24 inches, branched	.25	2.00

V. Opulus. HIGH-BUSH CRANBERRY. A tall shrub, with spreading branches. Flowers single white, produced in flat clusters in latter part of April. Berries scarlet; these remain all winter. Very showy.

	Each	10	100
3 to 4 feet, very bushy	$0.50	$4.00	
2 to 3 feet, well branched	.35	2.50	$20.00
18 to 24 inches, branched	.25	2.00	15.00

V. Opulus sterile. COMMON SNOWBALL. GUELDER ROSE. Produces large, globular clusters of white flowers in early April. An old favorite.

	Each	10	100
2 to 3 ft., heavy, well branched	$0.35	$3.00	$25.00
18 to 24 in., branched	.25	2.00	15.00

V. plicatum. JAPANESE SNOWBALL. A beautiful variety of upright, bushy growth; produces heads of white flowers in great profusion. Far superior to the old Snowball. Blooms early in April; lasts several weeks.

	Each	10
2 to 3 ft., heavy, well branched	$0.50	$4.00
18 to 24 in., branched	.35	3.00

Vitex. Chaste or Hemp Tree.

	Each	10
5 to 6 ft., very bushy	$0.75	$6.00
4 to 5 ft., very bushy	.50	4.00
3 to 4 ft., well branched	.35	3.00
2 to 3 ft., branched	.25	2.00

Vitex Agnus castus. This is a valuable shrub, or medium-growing tree. Flowers in spikes, lilac color, blooming early in May and lasting for a long time.

V. Agnus castus alba. Same as above, but with white flowers.

WHITE FRINGE. See Chionanthus.

Weigela. Diervilla.

Hardy, profuse-blooming shrubs of spreading habit. These are among the showiest of the garden shrubs, producing in early April great masses of showy flowers.

	Each	10	100
3 to 4 ft., bushy	$0.40	$3.00	
2 to 3 ft., well branched	.25	2.00	$15.00

Weigela candida. Pure white; excellent.

W. Eva Rathke. Flowers deep carmine-red; profuse bloomer and continues in bloom for a long time.

W. Gustav Mallet. The finest variety of its class; flowers light pink, margined white; very free bloomer.

W. rosea. Flowers are light pink, compact grower, free bloomer.

W. Van Houttei. Carmine; good grower.

Herbaceous Plants

Asclepias. Butterfly Weed.

Asclepias Tuberosa. SILKWEED. A very showy native plant, producing orange colored flowers during May and June.

	Each	10	100
Strong roots	$0.25	$2.00	$15.00

Chrysanthemums

Chrysanthemums, Hardy. We offer a most desirable collection of about 25 different varieties of Hardy Chrysanthemums, many of these being new sorts. All are named and of various colors—white, bronze, pink, yellow, crimson and all intermediate shades—both in the pompon and single-flowering sorts. These Chrysanthemums are most satisfactory in every way. They thrive in any good, rich garden soil and in full sunlight. They commence to bloom early in October and continue until frost.

	Each	10	100
Extra strong, field-grown clumps	$0.50	$4.00	$30.00
Strong, field-grown clumps	.25	2.00	15.00

Hibiscus

Hibiscus. MALLOW. Meehan's Mallow Marvels. Tall, hardy herbaceous plants, with very large and showy flowers. They thrive in any good, rich garden soil and in full sunlight. Throughout the entire summer they produce large, single flowers, sometimes 6 to 8 inches in diameter. We offer a fine lot, different assortment of sorts in white, flesh, pink, crimson and red.

	Each	10
Extra strong, 3-year roots	$0.35	$3.00
Strong, 2-year roots	.25	2.00

Iris

IRIS Germanica. GERMAN IRIS OR FLAG. The German Iris is one of our most desirable early spring-blooming plants. It is a vigorous grower and is of easy cultivation. Flowers are large and conspicuous. The colors are white, blue, purple, yellow, and variously veined and striped. Every garden should contain a collection of these Flags. Ten distinct. named varieties.

Strong roots, 15 cents each; $1.25 for 10; $10.00 per 100.

IRIS Kaempferi. JAPANESE IRIS. These handsome spring-blooming plants are becoming popular. They begin blooming about the middle of April and continue in bloom for five or six weeks. Many of the blooms have a diameter of from 8 to 12 inches, and are of various colors—white, purple, violet, mauve, magenta, variously marked and penciled. They are invaluable in herbaceous plantings, are extremely hardy and easily cultivated. Most effective where planted along the borders of ponds or streams. If the flower-stalks are cut just as the buds are expanding, and taken indoors, the flowers will last a long time, for as one flower fades another bud will open until all have shown their beautiful colors. With proper attention, this Iris will give a wealth of bloom and color. Twelve of the best named sorts.

25 cents each; $2.00 for 10; $17.50 per 100.

Peonies

PEONIES, Herbaceous. The varieties we offer have been thoroughly tested in this locality and have given most satisfactory results. We offer twelve to fifteen best sorts, double and single, white and several shades of pink, rose and red. Peonies do best in rich, rather moist, loamy soil, and if plants are protected from the hot afternoon sun, they will give excellent results. They should have a liberal supply of water at all times, especially when in bloom during April and May. Fertilize well with cow manure. Keep the ground well cultivated. If these few simple directions are carried out, the result will be most satisfactory. Plant during fall.

40 cents each; $3.50 for 10; $30.00 per 100.

Paeony.

AUGUSTA, GEORGIA.

Deciduous Trees

The intelligent tree planter readily appreciates the difference in value between a tree dug in the forest and one taken from our nursery where it has received proper care during the first years of its life. The one is tall, slender and with only a small top; the other is sturdy, with well-developed trunk and a top that is a promise of its future beauty and usefulness as a shade tree. All of our trees have been transplanted several times and plenty of room for development allowed in the row. The root-system is perfect, and, when our nursery-grown trees are properly set and pruned, there should be no loss.

Block of Hackberries.

Directions for Planting and Pruning. Before setting out, cut off the broken or bruised roots, should there be any. Trees with branching heads should have the smaller branches cut out, and the larger branches cut back to within three or four buds of their base; but, when a tree has an abundance of roots, and a small top, and few branches, then the pruning need not be so severe. However, when the roots are small and the top heavy, then prune the tree severely. In many cases remove every lateral limb, preserving only the leader, and this, if too long, may be cut back to the proper height. Frequently large trees are transplanted without pruning. This neglect will often cause the tree to die. Dig the hole intended for the tree of ample size, so when the young roots start out they will have soft ground in which to grow. The best fertilizer is well-rotted stable manure, thoroughly mixed with the soil.

Plant about two inches deeper than the tree originally stood in the nursery row, using the top soil for filling in around the roots. See that every interstice around the roots is thoroughly filled, and that every root is brought into contact with the soil. When the hole is nearly filled, pour in a bucket of water, so as to set the soil around the roots, then fill in the balance of the hole and press the dirt gently with the foot. When the tree is planted, mulch with five to six inches of well-decomposed stable manure; this should extend over the circumference of the hole. Keep free from grass and weeds, and loosen up the soil occasionally.

Acacia. Mimosa Tree.

Acacia Julibrissin. (*Albrizzia*). A rapid-growing tree, with spreading branches and a low, flat-topped head; foliage fine and feathery; pink flowers in large heads borne at tips of branches; blooms middle of May and continues for several weeks; a remarkably fine tree.

4 to 5 feet	$0.50	$4.00
2 to 3 feet	.25	2.00

Mimosa Tree.

Acer. Maple.

Acer dasycarpum, or saccharinum. SILVER OR WHITE MAPLE. A native species. A desirable, rapid-growing shade tree. Foliage bright green and silvery white beneath. Attains a height of 50 to 60 feet. Should not be confused with the Silver Poplar, or European Aspen, which throws up many shoots from the roots.

	Each	10	100
15-18 ft., specimens, 3-3½ in. cal.	$5.00	$40.00	
12-15 ft., 2-2½ in. cal.	2.00	15.00	$125.00
12-15 ft., 1¾-2 in. cal	1.50	10.00	80.00
10-12 ft., 1½-1¾ in. cal.	1.00	8.00	70.00
8-10 ft., 1¼-1½ in. cal	.75	6.00	45.00
8-10 ft., 1-1¼ in. cal	.50	4.00	30.00
6-8 ft., ¾-1 in. cal.	.40	3.00	25.00

A. Dasycarpum Wierii. WIER'S CUT-LEAF SILVER MAPLE. This is a beautiful form of the Silver Maple. Leaves deeply cut and delicately divided; branches drooping, frequently touching the ground. A rapid grower and a very effective and popular variety for lawn and park planting. Height, 35 to 40 feet.

	Each	10
8-10 ft., budded, well branched	$1.00	$8.00
6-8 ft., well branched	.75	6.00
5-6 ft., budded, well branched	.50	4.00

A. platanoides. NORWAY MAPLE. European species of compact and rapid growth; foliage deep, shining green. A most desirable shade tree. In many locali-

31

P. J. BERCKMANS CO.

ACER. MAPLE—Continued.

ties the Norway Maple is considered the best of all for street and park planting because of its sturdy growth, handsome form and beautiful foliage. Height, 40 to 50 feet.

	Each	10
10-12 ft., 1½-1¾ in. caliper	$2.00	
8-10 ft., 1¼-1½ in. caliper	1.25	$10.00
6-8 ft., stocky	.75	6.00

A. saccharum. SUGAR OR ROCK MAPLE. A magnificent variety for street and lawn. The tree assumes a dense habit of growth; foliage dark green, in autumn assuming beautiful shades of scarlet and yellow. Very hardy. Height, 50 to 60 feet.

	Each	10
10-12 ft., 1½-1¾ in., caliper	$2.00	
8-10 ft., 1¼-1½ in., caliper	1.25	$10.00
6-8 ft., stocky	.75	6.00

Acer Japonicum. Japanese Maple.

For many years it was considered impossible to grow Japanese Maples in this section, but where the trees are given the proper care and attention and planted in a shady situation where they are protected from the afternoon summer sun, these beautiful plants will give most satisfactory results. The Japanese Maples combine many attractive features, both in shape and color of foliage. The foliage is delicately and finely cut, and the decorative value of these Maples has long been recognized by all lovers of beautiful trees.

The best effect is secured by planting the various kinds in a bed; thus a pleasing color effect is given. For this purpose the plants should be set about 3 to 4 feet apart.

We offer about 10 or 12 of the best, most distinct and hardiest sorts.

	Each
3-4 ft., well branched, grafted	$3.00
2-3 ft., well branched, grafted	2.00
18-24 in., well branched, grafted	1.50

Aesculus. Horse Chestnut.

Æsculus rubicunda. RED-FLOWERING HORSE CHESTNUT. A very ornamental tree, attaining a height of 20 to 40 feet. Red flowers produced in large heads, which form a beautiful contrast with the deep green foliage. A great favorite.

	Each
2 to 3 feet, heavy	$0.50

Aleurites. Candle Nut.

Aleurites Fordii. CANDLE NUT OR CANDLE BERRY TREE. A medium size tree indigenous to Southeastern China. The tree attains a height of from 20 to 40 feet, and is extremely ornamental. The leaves are lobed and of a bright, shining green. In early spring it produces a mass of buff-colored flowers. The Walnut-like seeds make an oil which is variously known as Indian Walnut Oil, Kukui Oil, etc., which is largely used in the East for illuminating purposes. This tree is destined to become very popular for ornamental purposes; perfectly hardy at Augusta.

	Each	10
4 to 5 feet, very heavy	$1.00	$8.00
3 to 4 feet, heavy	.35	3.00	$25.00

Catalpa. Indian Bean.

Catalpa Bungeii. BUNGE'S CATALPA; UMBRELLA CATALPA. A darf variety from China. Foliage large and glossy. Makes an effective low-headed tree, somewhat like the Standard Bay in form. Very desirable for lawn planting and formal gardens. This Catalpa is usually grafted on stems 5 to 7 feet in height.

	Each
3 years, extra heavy, 5 to 7 feet, stems 2½ to 3 in. cal.	$2.50
3 years, extra heavy, 5 to 7 feet, stems 1½ to 2 in. cal.	2.00
2 years, extra heavy, 5 to 7 feet, stems 1¼ to 1½ in. cal.	1.50

Celtis. Hackberry.

Celtis Mississippiensis. NETTLE TREE, HACKBERRY OR SUGARBERRY. One of the most popular and desirable shade trees for avenue or street planting; of rapid growth. As the Hackberry is difficult to transplant, the tree must be pruned to a single stem, the roots kept moist and not exposed to the air, so that they will not dry out.

	Each	10	100
12 to 14 ft., well branched, 1½-2 in. cal.	$1.75	$15.00	
12 to 14 ft., well branched, 1¼-1½ in., cal.	1.50	12.50	$100.00
10 to 12 ft., well branched, 1-1¼ in., cal.	1.00	8.00	70.00
8 to 10 ft., stocky	.75	6.00	50.00
6 to 8 ft., stocky	.50	4.00	35.00

Cerasus. Flowering Cherry.

Cerasus avium flore plena alba. DOUBLE WHITE JAPANESE CHERRY. This is a remarkably fine tree. In early spring it produces a wealth of pure, double white flowers which are frequently so numerous that they conceal the branches; each individual flower resembles a miniature rose.

	Each	10	100
6-8 ft., heavy, well branched	$1.00		
5-6 ft., heavy, well branched	.75	$6.00	
4-5 ft., branched	.50	4.00	$30.00
3-4 ft., branched	.35	3.00	

C. Rhexi flore plena. Another very fine double white Japanese Cherry. Early in spring the tree is covered with a profusion of blooms; dwarf grower.

	Each	10
Strong, 2-year, 3-4 feet	$0.50	$4.00
2-3 ft.	.35	3.00

C. Japonica Rosea Pendula. JAPANESE WEEPING CHERRY. This is the well-known Weeping Cherry of the Japanese. In early spring the pendulous branches are covered with single rose-pink flowers in clusters, and the tree is literally a mass of bloom. The flowers appear before the leaves begin to unfold. A most desirable variety.

	Each
2-yr. heads, budded on 4 to 5 ft. stems	$1.50
1-yr. heads, budded on 4 to 5 ft. stems	1.25

Cercis. Judas Tree.

Cercis Canadensis. RED BUD OR AMERICAN JUDAS. A fast-growing round headed tree with large, leathery, heart-shaped leaves. The last of March, before the foliage appears, the tree is covered with a profusion of delicate reddish-purple flowers.

	Each	10	100
10 to 12 ft., 1¾ to 2¼ in., cal. extra heavy	$2.00	$17.50	
8 to 10 ft., 1½ to 1¾ in. cal., extra heavy	1.25	10.00	$90.00
6 to 8 ft., 1 to 1¼ in., cal.	1.00	8.00	70.00
5 to 6 ft., 1 in., cal.	.75	6.00	50.00
4 to 5 ft., stocky	.50	4.00	30.00

Aleurites Fordii, Candle Tree.

AUGUSTA, GEORGIA.

ive for several weeks after the blooming period. We recommend this tree highly. Height, 25 feet.

	Each	10
8 to 10 ft., heavy, well branched	$1.00	$8.00
6 to 8 ft., heavy, well branched	.75	6.00
5 to 6 ft., heavy, branched	.50	4.00

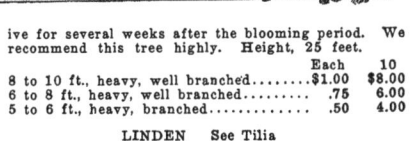

LINDEN See Tilia

Liquidambar. Sweet Gum.

Liquidambar styraciflua. AMERICAN SWEET GUM, OR BILSTED. One of our handsome native trees. Of upright and symmetrical growth. Especially showy in autumn, when the leaves change from green to either yellow or deep purple. Invaluable for street and landscape planting.

	Each	10
8-10 ft., heavy, 1¼ to 1½ in. cal.	$1.50	$12.50
6-8 ft., heavy, 1 to 1¼ in. cal.	1.00	8.00
5-6 ft., heavy	.75	6.00
4-5 ft., stocky	.50	4.00

Liriodendron. Tulip Poplar.

Liriodendron tulipifera. TULIP TREE; TULIP POPLAR. A magnificent, rapid-growing tree of pyramidal shape; foliage broad and glossy; flowers yellowish-green, tulip-shaped. Valuable for street and lawn planting; also for lumber. Needs severe pruning when transplanted.

	Each	10	100
15-18 ft., 3 to 3½ in. cal.	$3.50	$30.00	$250.00
12-15 ft., 2 to 2½ in cal.	2.00	17.50	150.00
10-12 ft., 1¾ to 2 in. cal.	1.25	10.00	90.00
8-10 ft., 1¼ to 1¾ in. cal.	1.00	8.00	70.00
6- 8 ft., 1 to 1¼ in. cal.	.75	6.00	50.00
5- 6 ft., 1 in. cal.	.50	4.00	35.00

Magnolia. Chinese Species.

All of the Chinese varieties produce their flowers in the early spring, before the leaves appear, and several sorts produce, or continue to bloom, at periods during the entire summer. No selection is complete without some of these desirable plants.

Magnolia Purpurea. (M. Obovata). CHINESE PURPLE MAGNOLIA. This popular variety makes a small tree of compact growth; large purple and white flowers are produced in great profusion the latter part of March, and a few flowers are produced during the entire summer.

Red-Flowering Dogwood and Deodara Cedar.

Cornus. Dogwood.

Cornus florida. WHITE-FLOWERING DOGWOOD. The native large white-flowering Dogwood. A most effective plant for the lawn.

	Each	10
4 to 5 ft., very heavy	$0.75	$6.00
3 to 4 ft., well branched	.50	4.00
2 to 3 ft., branched	.35	3.00

C. florida flore rubra. RED-FLOWERING DOGWOOD. Similar to the White-flowering Dogwood, but the flowers are of a deep rose color. Early in the season it produces large quantities of flowers, which makes it a most effective tree.

	Each	10
4 to 5 ft., very heavy, budded	$2.50	
3 to 4 ft., heavy, budded	1.50	
2 to 3 ft., stocky, budded	1.00	$8.00

CRAB APPLE, DOUBLE-FLOWERING
See Malus spectabilis

ELM. See Ulmus

HORSE-CHESTNUT. See Aesculus.

Koelreuteria

Koelreuteria paniculata. GOLDEN RAIN TREE. A most beautiful, hardy, ornamental shade tree from China, with broad, flat, spreading head of large compound-ovate leaves, which are of a dull red when first appearing in the spring, later assuming a dark-bright green. During the latter part of May large panicles of orange-yellow flowers are produced for at least three weeks. These completely envelop the entire head of the tree. The flowers are followed by bladder-like seed pods, which make the tree very attract-

Koelreuteria paniculata.

P. J. BERCKMANS CO.

Magnolia Soulangeana.

MAGNOLIA—continued.

	Each	10
6 to 8 ft., very bushy specimens	$3.50	$30.00
5 to 6 ft., very bushy specimens	2.50	22.50
4 to 5 ft., very bushy	1.50	12.50
3 to 4 ft., well branched	1.00	8.00
2 to 3 ft., well branched	.75	6.00
18 to 24 in., branched	.50	4.00

M. Soulangeana. SOULANGE'S MAGNOLIA. The illustration of this beautiful Magnolia on this page will give an idea of the magnificence of this hardy tree. Flowers large, cup-shaped; white, more or less suffused with pink. Blooms in March. Hardy. Ultimate height, 25 feet.

	Each.
3 to 4 ft., well budded, imported	$2.50
3 to 3½ ft., well branched, with buds; imported	1.50
2 to 3 ft., branched, with buds; imported	1.00

M. Soulangeana nigra. DARK-FLOWERED MAGNOLIA. A very rare variety of vigorous and robust growth; flowers large, dark purple; several shades darker than M. Purpurea. A free bloomer. Commences to bloom in March and blooms spasmodically during the entire summer. A most beautiful and desirable variety. Distinct from any other sort.

	Each.
8 to 10 ft., very bushy specimens	$5.00
6 to 8 ft., bushy	3.50

M. stellata (*M. Halleana*). STARRY MAGNOLIA. Of dwarf habit. Flowers semi-double, pure white, and fragrant. Blooms from two to three weeks earlier than other Magnolias.

	Each.
2 to 3 feet, beautiful specimens, well budded	$2.50
18 to 24 in., branched, well budded	1.50

Malus. Apple.

Malus spectabilis. DOUBLE-FLOWERING CHINESE CRAB APPLE. A small-sized tree, producing double, pink flowers. Very handsome in bloom.

	Each.	10
5 to 6 ft., heavy, well branched	$0.50	$4.00
4 to 5 ft.	.25	2.00

Melia. China Tree.

Melia Azedarach umbraculiformis. TEXAS UMBRELLA TREE; UMBRELLA CHINA. A sub-variety of the China Tree. It assumes a dense, spreading head, resembling a gigantic umbrella. A most desirable tree of rapid growth. Blooms middle of April. Ultimate height, 25 feet.

	Each	10	100
8-10 ft. specimens, 3 to 3½ in. cal.	$3.50	$30.00	
7 to 8 ft., heavy, well branched, 1¾ to 2¼ in. cal.	2.00	17.50	
6 to 7 ft., heavy, branched, 1¼ to 1¾ in. cal.	1.00	8.00	$60.00
5 to 6 ft., well branched, 1 to 1¼ in. cal.	.75	6.00	50.00
4 to 5 ft., branched, 1 in. cal.	.50	4.00	30.00
3 to 4 ft	.25	2.00	17.50

Morus. Mulberry.

Morus alba pendula. TEAS WEEPING MULBERRY. A beautiful and hardy Weeping Mulberry. Forms a perfect umbrella-shaped head, with long, slender, willowy branches drooping to the ground. Desirable for lawn, parks or cemeteries.

	Each.	10
Extra heavy, 3-year heads, budded on 5 to 7 ft. stems, 1½ to 2 in. cal.	$2.00	$15.00
Heavy, 2-year heads, budded on 5 to 7 ft. stems, 1¼ to 1½ in. cal.	1.25	10.00
Strong, 2-year heads, budded on 5 to 7 ft. stems, 1 in. cal.	1.00	8.00

OAK. See Quercus

Oxydendron. Sourwood.

Oxydendron arboreum. SOURWOOD. A small tree, with slender, spreading branches, growing naturally from Pennsylvania to Louisiana. Leaves lanceolate, bright green. In autumn assumes dazzling tones of scarlet. Fragrant white flowers in panicles or spreading racemes. Blooms in early summer. Ultimate height, 25 to 50 feet.

	Each.	10
2 to 3 feet	$0.35	$3.00

Persica. Peach. Double Flowering.

During March these Double-Flowering Peaches are covered with a mass of beautifully formed and highly colored flowers. These trees cannot be too highly recommended for early spring blooming. They are perfectly hardy and will thrive on any soil in which other Peaches will grow.

	Each.	10
1 year, extra heavy	$0.50	$4.00
1 year, 3-4 ft., well branched	.35	3.00

Persica chrysanthemum. CHRYSANTHEMUM-FLOWERED PEACH. Flowers large, double, pink center quilled like a chrysanthemum. Extra fine, new variety.

Texas Umbrella.

34

AUGUSTA, GEORGIA.

PERSICA—Continued.

Double Crimson Peach.
Double Pink Peach.
Double White Peach.

Platanus. Plane Tree.

Platanus occidentalis. AMERICAN SYCAMORE. The well-known variety. It is extensively used for street and park planting, especially where there is smoke. Ultimate height, 100 to 150 feet.

	Each	10	100
12 to 14 ft., 2-2½ in. cal. well-branched	$2.00		
10 to 12 ft., 1¼-1½ in. cal. well-branched	1.00	$8.00	$70.00
8 to 10 ft., well-branched	.75	6.00	50.00
6 to 8 ft., well-branched	.50	4.00	30.00

Populus. Poplar.

Populus Caroliniensis. CAROLINA POPLAR. A rapid-growing native tree of upright growth. After the tree has attained a height of 15 to 20 feet, it is advisable to cut the leader. This will cause the tree to make a spreading head. The Carolina Poplar resembles the Cottonwood, but is quite distinct.

	Each	10	100
12 to 14 ft., 1½-2 in., cal.	$1.00	$8.00	
10 to 12 ft., 1¼-1½ in. cal.	.60	5.00	$40.00
8 to 10 ft., 1-1¼ in., cal.	.50	4.00	30.00
6 to 8 ft., ¾-1 in. cal.	.25	2.25	20.00

P. Fastigiata. (*P. Nigra*). LOMBARDY POPLAR. The well-known Italian variety. A tall, pyramidal, compact and rapid-growing tree; very hardy; extensively planted in the southern part of Europe. Very desirable where formal effect is desired.

	Each	10	100
8 to 10 ft., 1-1½ inch. cal.	$0.50	$4.00	$30.00
6 to 8 ft., ¾ to 1 inch. cal.	.25	2.25	20.00

P. Simoni. (*Balsamifera Suaveolens*). CHINESE POPLAR. A remarkable new variety of the small-leaf Chinese Poplar of very pyramidal habit; resembles the Lombardy, but makes a more pleasing impression; a very rapid grower, and is destined to become a popular variety. Introduced by the Horticultural explorer, Mr. Frank N. Meyer.

	Each	10	100
10 to 12 ft., 1¼-1½ inch cal.	$1.00	$8.00	
8 to 10 ft., 1-1¼ inch. cal.	.75	6.00	$40.00
6 to 8 ft.	.50	4.00	30.00

POUPARTIA. See Spondias axillaris.

Prunus. Plum.

Prunus Mume. JAPANESE DOUBLE-FLOWERING APRICOT. A very early-blooming variety. In March the tree is literally covered with a mass of double pink blossoms, making a most conspicuous tree for a lawn. Very scarce.

	Each.	10
Strong, 1-year trees	$0.50	$4.00

P. Pissardi. PERSIAN PURPLE-LEAF PLUM. The most valuable of all the purple-leaved trees. It retains its deep color throughout the warmest weather, and its leaves until midwinter. We cannot endorse it too highly.

	Each	10
4 to 5 ft., heavy	$0.50	$4.00
3 to 4 ft., strong	.25	2.00

P. Vesuvius. Originated by Luther Burbank. This variety is somewhat like Prunus Pissardii, the Purple-leaved Plum, but is superior in every way. Its fruit is of a deep, rich color with a pleasant, acid flavor; not a very prolific bearer, but is more desirable as an ornamental tree on account of its gigantic crimson-colored leaves. Tree a vigorous grower.

	Each	10
4 to 5 ft., 1 yr., budded	$0.50	$4.00

Quercus. The Oak.

All of our Oaks have been several times transplanted, and therefore have a good root system; but, nevertheless, all Oaks must be severely pruned when transplanted; otherwise there is danger of the trees dying.

Quercus nigra. (*Quercus aquatica*). WATER OAK. This well-known variety needs no description.

	Each	10
14-16 ft. specimens, 3½ to 4 in. cal.	$6.00	
12 to 14 ft. very heavy, 2 to 2½ in. cal.	3.00	
10 to 12 ft. very heavy, 1½ to 2 in. cal.	1.50	$12.50
8 to 10 ft. heavy, well-branched, 1¼ to 1½ in. cal.	1.25	10.00
6 to 8 ft. heavy, well-branched, 1 in. cal.	.75	6.00
5 to 6 ft. heavy, well-branched.	.50	4.00

Q. palustris. PIN OAK. The tree is shapely and symmetrical; leaves are of a beautiful tone of green, in autumn fading to a brilliant scarlet. This is one of the most desirable trees for street and avenue planting. Ultimate height, 50 to 60 feet.

	Each	
18-20 ft., specimens, 5 to 6 in. cal.	$15.00	to $20.00
15-18 ft., specimens, 3½ to 4 in. cal.	5.00	to 7.50
12-15 ft., specimens, 2½ to 3½ in. cal.	4.00	to 5.00

	Each	10
10-12 ft., 1¾ to 2 in. cal, very heavy	$2.00	$17.50
8-10 ft. 1½ to 1¾ in cal	1.50	12.50
6-8 ft., 1 to 1¼ in. cal.	1.00	9.00

Q. phellos. WILLOW OAK. A very graceful variety, with narrow lanceolate leaves, resembling those of the willow. Well-known native tree, but extremely difficult to secure.

	Each
10 to 12 ft., 1½ to 2 in. cal.	$1.50
8 to 10 ft., 1¼ to 1½ in cal	1.25
6 to 8 ft., heavy, well branched	.75
5 to 6 ft., heavy, well branched	.50

Salisburia. Ginkgo.

Salisburia adiantifolia. (*Ginkgo Biloba*.) MAIDENHAIR TREE. A most beautiful and interesting Japanese tree. Of large size, rapid and erect growth. Foliage resembles that of the Maidenhair Fern. One of the most desirable shade trees we have. Free from insect diseases. A very popular tree in many cities for street and avenue planting. Considerably used in Washington, D. C. Ultimate height, 60 to 80 feet.

	Each	10
8 to 10 feet	$1.25	$10.00
6 to 8 feet	.75	6.50
5 to 6 feet	.50	4.00

Salix. Willow.

Salix Japonica. JAPANESE WEEPING WILLOW. Being an improvement on Salix Babylonica, as it puts out its leaves about ten days later in the spring, which thus prevents it from the injuries of late frost.

	Each	10	100
10 to 12 ft., very heavy, 1¾ to 2 in.	$1.50	$12.50	
8 to 10 ft., very heavy	1.00	6.00	
6 to 8 ft., heavy	.50	3.00	$25.00
5 to 6 ft., well branched	.25	2.00	15.00

Spondias Axillaris.

Spondias axillaris. (*Poupartia*). A new deciduous shade tree, introduced from China by the Horticultural Explorer, Mr. Wilson. This is a most valuable addition to our collection of hardy deciduous trees. The tree grows from 40 to 75 feet high, with a trunk 3 feet in diameter. The branches are massive and form an oval or round head. The bark is gray and deeply fissured. Insignificant flowers are borne in clusters, followed by oval fruit about an inch long. The fruit is eaten by the Chinese. We are glad to have the opportunity of offering this rare tree.

	Each	10
6 to 8 ft., very heavy	$1.00	
5 to 6 ft., heavy	.75	$6.00
4 to 5 ft.	.50	4.00

35

P. J. BERCKMANS CO.

Sterculia. Varnish Tree.

Sterculia platanifolia. VARNISH TREE; JAPAN PARASOL. A very desirable shade tree of rapid growth. Large panicles of yellowish-white flowers in June. Leaves large; bark very smooth and green. Fine tree for bees. Height, 40 to 50 feet.

	Each	10
10 to 12 ft., extra heavy, 1¾ to 2 in. cal.	$2.00	$15.00
8 to 10 ft., very heavy, 1½ to 1¾ in. c	1.50	10.00
6 to 8 alft., heavy	1.00	8.00
4 to 6 ft., heavy	.75	6.00

SOURWOOD. See Oxydendron

SWEET GUM. See Liquidambar

Taxodium. Bald Cypress.

Taxodium distichum. BALD CYPRESS OF THE SOUTH. The native Cypress of the South. Foliage soft green, light and feathery; in the autumn the color is yellow and orange; does well in moist or dry soil; a magnificent deciduous tree, and for avenue or park effect is most pleasing. This tree is not sufficiently appreciated.

	Each	10
8 to 10 ft., very heavy	$2.00	
6 to 8 ft., very heavy	1.50	$12.50
5 to 6 ft., very heavy	1.00	8.00
4 to 5 ft., heavy	.75	6.00
3 to 4 ft., heavy	.50	4.00

Tilia. Linden.

Tilia Americana. AMERICAN LINDEN, OR LIME. A handsome and desirable, large-sized tree of rapid growth. Indigenous from Canada to Texas. Leaves heart-shaped, dark green, in autumn turning to a golden hue. Most desirable for street planting. Succeeds best in rich soil.

	Each	10
8 to 10 ft., 1¼-1½ inch. cal.	$1.50	$12.50
6 to 8 ft.	1.00	8.00

TULIP TREE. See Liriodendron

Ulmus. Elm.

Ulmus Americana. AMERICAN WHITE ELM. A native tree of rapid and stately growth. Branches long and graceful. Extensively used for avenues and streets. We have an exceptionally fine stock of symmetrical and stocky trees.

	Each	10	100
12 to 14 ft., 1½-1¾ in. cal.	$1.50	$12.50	
10 to 12 ft., 1¼-1½ in. cal.	1.00	8.00	$70.00
8 to 10 ft., 1-1¼ in. cal.	.75	6.00	50.00
6 to 8 ft., ¾ in caliper.	.50	4.00	35.00

UMBRELLA CHINA. See Melia

Virgilia. Cladrastis.

Virgilia lutea. YELLOW WOOD. A medium-sized tree with spreading, somewhat pendulous branches, with a symmetrical round head. Leaves bright green, turning golden early in autumn. In early spring white flowers are produced in loose, drooping panicles. A desirable lawn tree.

	Each
10-12 ft., heavy, well branched	$1.50
8-10 ft., heavy, well branched	1.25

WEEPING MULBERRY. See Morus

WILLOW. See Salix

Broad Leaved Evergreens.

We can supply large specimen plants of many varieties of Broad-leaved Evergreens described in this catalogue. Descriptions, prices and sizes will be given to prospective purchasers. All of our plants are most carefully grown, frequently transplanted, pruned and given plenty of space; therefore the plants which are offered are stately, vigorous and healthy.

Many of our evergreens are grown in pots, thereby increasing safety in transplanting. In fact, it is impossible to transplant some varieties of Broad-leaved Evergreens which have been grown in open ground; therefore, to make the transplanting of these particular varieties assured, we grow them in pots.

Nearly all plants which are taken from the open ground are lifted with a ball of earth about the roots. This is wrapped in moss, excelsior or burlap. When transplanting evergreens which have a ball of earth about the roots and same wrapped in burlap, it is not necessary to remove this burlap. Place the plant to the right depth in the properly prepared hole; cut the string so that the burlap can be released from about the ball of earth around the roots of the plant. It is not necessary to remove the burlap from the hole, but when the ball of earth about the roots of the plant is wrapped in moss or excelsior this wrapping must be carefully removed, but the earth about the roots should not be disturbed. When the hole has been half-filled with earth, pour in water freely, but not so as to wash the soil from about the roots of the plant. After the water has settled put in more dirt and firm this well about the roots of the plant, and then fill up the hole.

In transplanting broad-leaved evergreens the soil should be properly prepared and holes of ample size dug and fertilized. In all cases the fertilizer must be thoroughly incorporated with the soil. If the roots of the plants come in contact with the unmixed manure the plants are apt to die. Should the ball of earth about the roots of broad-leaved evergreens fall away, then the plant must be defoliated and properly pruned. Even when the ball of earth about the roots of plants remains intact it is advisable to prune some evergreens slightly, such as: Abelia, Cerasus Caroliniana, Camphor, Cotoneaster, Crataegus, Elaeagnus, Ilex, Laurocerasus, Ligustrum, Nerium.

It is advisable to place a mulching of well-rotted leaves to a depth of 4 to 6 inches about the plants, as this mulching conserves the moisture in the soil, and the roots are protected from the sudden changes of temperature. In the summer the mulching prevents drying out of the soil, and in winter freezing.

We are beginning to appreciate more and more the effect attained by a proper planting and selection of Broad-leaved Evergreens. We are particularly fortunate in being able to grow in this favored locality such a large collection of Broad-leaved Evergreens. We can successfully grow in this section many kinds which are not hardy in the far North, and we also bring to perfection a large portion of the hardy northern Evergreens. A judicious selection of varieties, with the proper planting arrangement of Evergreen trees and shrubs, gives to the winter aspect of our home grounds a warm and cheerful effect. Of course, certain varieties require specially prepared soil; otherwise they will not give satisfactory results.

At all times we would be pleased to give suggestions as to the best varieties for certain localities.

It is advisable to defoliate nearly all Broad-leaved Evergreens which are lifted from the open ground. This will lessen the loss by transplanting. Many varieties do not transplant well if moved with all the leaves left on. This is especially applicable to Magnolias, Photinias, Crataegus, Ligustrums, Cerasus, Elaegnus, English Laurel, the Evergreen Oaks and Viburnums. It is also advisable to properly prune these plants as soon as they are transplanted.

All broad-leaved evergreens are pot-grown unless otherwise stated.

PRICES OF SPECIAL COLLECTIONS

We will supply 10 plants in 10 varieties, our selection, standard sizes, for .... $ 4.00
100 plants in 25 varieties, our selection, stand ard sizes, for 25.00

NOTE—The two above special collections are of fine value.

AUGUSTA, GEORGIA.

Abelia grandiflora.

Abelia

Abelia grandiflora. (*A. rupestris*). One of our most beautiful, popular and satisfactory broad-leaved evergreens. The graceful, drooping stems and branches are covered with dark, glossy leaves which in winter assume a metalic sheen. From the last of May until frost this plant produces an immense quantity of tubular-shaped white flowers about an inch long, which are borne in clusters. The accompanying photo will give an idea of the beauty of the Abelia. During the growing season it is advisable to pinch off the ends of the long shoots. This will make the plant dense and compact. For single specimens, for groups, or for a hedge we cannot too strongly recommend this plant.

	Each	10	100
2 to 3 ft., strong plants, from open ground	$0.75	$5.00	$40.00
18 to 24 in., strong, from open ground	.50	4.00	30.00
12 to 18 in., strong, from open ground	.35	3.00	25.00

Arbutus. Strawberry Tree.

Arbutus Unedo. STRAWBERRY TREE. A very rare and desirable broad-leaved evergreen. Attains a height of 8 to 15 feet. Foliage dark, glossy green. Flowers white, bell-shaped, produced in early spring in great profusion, followed by pretty scarlet fruit, which is retained until late winter.

	Each	10
18-24 in., strong, from pots	$1.00	
15-18 in., strong, from pots	.75	$6.00
12-15 in., strong, from pots	.60	5.00
10-12 in., strong, from pots	.50	4.00

Ardisia

Ardisia crenulata rubra. An exceedingly ornamental dwarf-growing shrub, with dark, shining leaves; produces a profusion of bright-red berries which remain upon the plant for a year. Succeeds best in a shady situation, and in a rich soil. Hardy at Savannah and southward. This plant is very largely used as a house plant in winter.

	Each	10
10 to 12 in. from 4 in. pots, well set with berries	$1.00	
8 to 10 in., from 4 in. pots, well set with berries	.75	$6.00
6 to 8 in. from 3½ and 4 in. pots, well set with berries	.50	4.00
8 to 10 in. from 4 in pots, without berries	.60	5.00
6 to 8 in. from 4 in. pots, without berries	.35	3.00

Aucuba. Gold Dust Tree.

This genus contains both male and female plants. If the latter are planted near the male plants, they produce a profusion of red berries which makes them very attractive. Succeeds best in shady situation and in a somewhat moist, though rich, well-drained soil. The Aucubas are largely used for vases, urns and window boxes.

PRICES, except where noted. All plants from open ground.

	Each	10	100
5 t 6 ft., very bushy	$5.00		
36 to 40 inches, well branched	1.50		
2 to 3 ft., well branched	1.00	$8.00	
18 to 24 inches, well branched	.75	6.00	
12 to 18 inches, branched	.50	4.00	30.00

Aucuba Himalaica. A strong growing variety with large, dark, glossy leaves. Produces a profusion of scarlet berries which makes a fine contrast with the rich, green foliage.

A. Japonica. A beautiful variety of dwarf growth. Leaves narrow, dark, shining green; produces a profusion of bright red berries, which remain upon the plant for a long time. Very desirable for growing in pots as well as for open ground.

	Each	10
24 to 30 inches, bushy	$1.50	
18 to 24 inches, well branched	1.00	$8.00
12 to 18 inches, branched	.75	6.00
10 to 12 inches, branched	.50	4.00

P. J. BERCKMANS CO.

AUCUBA—Continued.

A. Japonica aureo-maculata. GOLD-DUST TREE. A form of the above, with leaves beautifully spotted with yellow. Largely used for jardinieres and window-boxes; also for planting in masses.

Azalea

Azalea amoena. EARLY AMOENA. A very dwarf-growing variety, producing small, claret-colored blooms. Excellent for a low hedge or for massing. Hardy at New York.

	Each	10	100
15 to 18 inches, very bushy, with buds, from open ground	$1.00	$8.00	$70.00
12 to 15 in., very bushy, with buds, from open ground	.75	6.00	55.00
10 to 12 in., very bushy, from open ground	.50	4.00	35.00
8 to 10 in., bushy	.40	3.50	25.00
6 to 8 in., well branched	.30	2.50	20.00

A. Hinodegiri. A magnificent, hardy, early-blooming Japanese Azalea; decided improvement upon A. amoena, which it somewhat resembles in habit of growth, but is a more vigorous grower and foliage is heavier. Bright carmine flowers are produced in enormous quantities. In fact, when in full bloom, the plant is almost a solid mass of color. Remains in bloom for a long period. In the winter and fall months the foliage assumes a reddish appearance. This variety is hardy in New York.

	Each	10
10 to 12 in., very bushy, well set with buds	$1.00	$8.00
8 to 10 in., very bushy, well set with buds	.75	6.00
6 to 8 in., well branched, with buds	.50	4.00

Azalea Indica. Indian Azaleas.

(Home Grown)

	Each	10	100
18 to 24 in., very bushy, well set with buds	$1.00		
15 to 18 in., very bushy, well set with buds	.75	$6.00	$55.00
12 to 15 in., branched, well set with buds	.50	4.00	35.00
8 to 12 in., branched, with buds	.40	3.50	25.00
6 to 8 in., branched with buds	.30	2.50	20.00

These beautiful shrubs are perfectly hardy in this latitude, but give the best results when planted in a somewhat shady situation, especially where they are protected from the hot afternoon sun of summer.

The best soil is one containing an abundance of leaf mold, peat and sand.

The plants should be kept well mulched with rotted leaves. Azaleas are always desirable, either for massing or as single specimens in the open ground, or for the decoration of conservatories or houses.

If the plants are grown in pots, they should be repotted after flowering and before the new growth begins. Keep the plants sheltered for a few days, and then plunge the pots in the open ground in a shady situation, or they may be planted in an open border and kept shaded.

If the plants are required for winter blooming in the conservatory, they should be lifted and repotted before very cold weather and kept in a cool greenhouse. By judiciously selecting the varieties, a continuous supply of flowers may be had from January until May.

We offer several thousand Home-grown Indian Azaleas in about 50 varieties of the sizes as described above. In the varieties with single flowers we offer all shades of crimson, scarlet, purple, salmon, white, and many exquisitely variegated, mottled and striped varieties. In the varieties with double flowers we can only supply two double whites. All our plants are grown in open ground during summer and lifted and potted in October when they are thoroughly matured. In this latitude it is best to plant Azaleas in open ground in March, but southward they can be safely planted from October until April.

Azaleas are liable to attacks of red spider and thrips, especially if the plants suffer from want of proper watering. Daily syringing of plants kept under glass will aid in eradicating these pests, as also will a spray of sulpho-tobacco soap.

Potting soil should be composed of half peat, half leaf-mold and good loam; abundant drainage must be given.

A well-fed, well-tended and well-pruned Azalea need never grow scraggy and misshapen with age, but should become more beautiful every year, as its increasing spread of branches gives room for the display of myriads more of flowers. Those who grow Azaleas in the house should remember that the flowers will last much longer if the plants are kept in a cool room after they have expanded.

Berberis Barberry.

Berberis Japonica. (*Mahonia Japonica*). JAPANESE BARBERRY. This splendid plant thrives in almost any situation, but does best in a partially shaded location, where the ground is well drained. Leaves very broad, with five pairs of leaflets; flowers yellow in long spikes during the first three months of the year, followed by dark purple berries. A magnificent shrub.

	Each	10	100
24 to 30 in., very heavy, open ground	$1.25	$10.00	
18 to 24 in., heavy, open ground	.75	6.00	$50.00
12 to 18 in., heavy, open ground	.50	4.00	35.00
10 to 12 in., heavy, open ground	.40	3.00	25.00

Buxus. Boxwood.

Buxus Balearica. A very handsome variety of Boxwood; a native of Spain. Large, oblong, bright-shining leaves 1 to 2 inches in length. Not hardy in the North.

Berberis Japonica.

Azalea

AUGUSTA, GEORGIA.

BUXUS—Continued.

	Each	10	100
24 to 30 in., bushy, open ground	$0.75	$6.00	
18 to 24 in., bushy, open ground	.60	5.00	
12 to 18 in., bushy, open ground	.50	4.00	$30.00

B. Handsworthi. A stiff-leaved, upright form of Boxwood, with large, dark green leaves. Very hardy and distinct.

	Each	10
18 to 24 in., very bushy	$0.75	$6.00
12 to 18 in., bushy	.50	4.00

B. Sempervirens. TREE BOX. Imported. Untrimmed bushes. A large shrub of compact habit. This old plant is again in great favor and is being extensively planted. We offer a fine lot of very compact, bushy plants.

	Each	10	100
2 ft., by 15 in., spread, very compact, open ground	$1.50		
18 in. by 10 in., spread, very compact, open ground	1.00	$8.00	
12 in. by 10 in. spread, very compact, open ground	.50	4.50	$40.00

B. Sempervirens. (Home-grown). We offer a fine lot of compact, thrifty plants.

	Each	10	100
18 to 24 in., very bushy, from open ground	$0.75	$6.00	
15 to 18 in., very bushy, from open ground	.50	4.00	$30.00
12 to 15 in., very bushy, from open ground	.40	3.00	25.00

For smaller sizes, see under Hedge Plants.

B. Sempervirens aurea variegata. A form of Buxus sempervirens with leaves margined yellow.

	Each	10
10 to 12 inches	$0.50	$4.00

B. suffruticosa. DWARF BOXWOOD. See under head of Hedge Plants. Page 49.

Boxwood, Pyramidal
Trimmed.

These are very popular for decorative purposes, as they can be utilized in exposed places where the temperature is too low for palms. We offer a beautiful lot of imported specimens.

	Each
4 ft. by 18-20 in. diameter	$5.00
3½ ft. by 16-18 in. diameter	4.00
3 ft. by 15-18 in. diameter	3.00
2½ ft. by 12-15 in. diameter	1.50

Camellia Japonica. Home Grown Plants.

The Camellia is one of our specialties. We have of our own growing several thousand healthy, vigorous plants. The demand for this old favorite is continually increasing. All of our plants are propagated from our own specimens, which are grown in open ground. Our collection contains nearly 100 choice varieties, and the plants we offer comprise a great range of colors; also early and late-blooming varieties, with double and semi-double blooms.

	Each	10	100
15 to 18 in., slightly branched	$1.00	$8.00	
12 to 15 in., slightly branched	.75	6.50	
12 to 15 in., not branched	.50	4.50	$40.00

Camellia Japonica. Imported Plants.

Imported Camellias will be extremely scarce this year. Fortunately, we have a limited quantity from last year's importation. These plants are in fine condition. We can supply red, pink, white, crimson and many beautiful variegated sorts. These Camellias are from reliable European growers, but we cannot guarantee that every plant of the colored varieties will come true to label. We purchase under these conditions, and we

Pyramidal Box.

have to sell under the same conditions; furthermore, some of the varieties of variegated Camellias will frequently produce, on the same plant, white, variegated, pink or red blooms.

	Each
24 to 30 in., well-branched	$3.00
18 to 24 in., well-branched	2.00
15 to 18 in., well-branched	1.50

CULTIVATION OF CAMELLIAS.

For Open Ground—A partially shaded situation, especially where protected from the cold winds of winter, is most desirable. Any good garden soil is suitable, but if mixed with leaf-mold, better results will be obtained. Keep the plants thoroughly mulched with well-rotted leaves. The best time to transplant Camellias in this section is from early October to the middle of November, and from the middle of February to the end of March.

For Conservatories—Use a potting compost of peat or leaf-mold and good loam, and give ample drainage. When in growth, they require an abundance of water and spraying of the foliage. When dormant, water sparingly and keep in cool temperature. Fire heat is not needed except during excessively cold weather which would injure distending buds. Dropping of buds is caused by plants drying out, or by over-watering, or being kept in high temperature under glass.

CAPE JASMINE. See Gardenia

39

P. J. BERCKMANS CO.

Cerasus. Carolina Cherry.

Cerasus Caroliniana. (*Prunus Caroliniana*). MOCK ORANGE OF THE SOUTH. This well-known hardy evergreen can be safely classed as a tree, as it attains a height from 20 to 40 feet. It is very desirable as a single specimen or for grouping, as it makes a most effective background in landscape work. Can also be pruned in standard, pyramidal, and other formal shapes. We offer a fine stock of thrifty, transplanted plants. As the Carolina Cherry is difficult to transplant, it is always advisable to defoliate and cut back severely, and unless authorized to the contrary all plants will be so treated before shipment.

	Each	10	100
3 to 4 ft. heavy, very bushy, open ground	$1.00	$8.00	
2 to 3 ft. heavy, well-branched, open ground	.50	4.00	$30.00
18 to 24 inches, well-branched, open ground	.35	3.00	25.00
12 to 18 inches, well-branched, open ground	.25	2.00	17.50

Chamaerops. Palm.

Chamaerops Canariensis. CANARY ISLAND PALM. A very graceful variety, with deeply-cut, fan-shaped leaves; hardy at Augusta and southward.

	Each	10
18 to 24 inches	$0.75	$6.00
15 to 18 inches	.50	4.00

C. Fortunei. (*C. Excelsa*). CHUSAN FAN PALMETTO. This is without doubt the hardiest of all exotic palms. Easily stands zero weather without injury. Fine specimens are grown in the northern part of South Carolina and Georgia. The plant attains a height of 12 to 15 feet. Seems to adapt itself to a great variety of soils, but will give best results when grown in a rich, heavy, well-drained soil. Very graceful and ornamental.

	Each	10	100
3½ to 4-ft. specimens	$4.00		
30 to 36 in., extra heavy	3.00		
24 to 30 in., extra heavy	2.00	$18.00	
18 to 24 in., extra heavy	1.00	8.00	$70.00
15 to 18 in., strong	.75	6.00	55.00
12 to 15 in., strong	.50	4.00	35.00

Cinnamomum. Camphor.

Cinnamomum Camphora. THE CAMPHOR TREE. This beautiful tree might be safely classed as hardy at Augusta, as it is rarely injured by frost. In central Georgia there are some magnificent trees 30 years old. Along the Atlantic and Gulf States it is used as a shade tree for street and avenue planting. The

Chamaerops Fortunei.

Camphor.

Camphor is of very rapid and stately growth. Leaves bright, glossy green. The young growth is tinged red, which gives a most striking and pleasing effect. The Camphor will do well on poor soil, but will give a more satisfactory growth when properly fertilized and grown on well-drained ground. In Florida the Camphor is now being extensively and successfully planted for commercial purposes. In transplanting, both the pot-grown and open ground plants should have their side branches cut back and the plants defoliated.

	Each	10	100
4 to 5 ft., well-branched, pot-grown	$1.00	$7.00	$60.00
3 to 4 ft., well-branched, pot-grown	.75	5.00	45.00
30 to 36 inches, well-branched, pot-grown	.50	3.50	30.00
24 to 30 inches, well-branched, pot-grown	.35	2.50	20.00
18 to 24 inches, branched, pot-grown	.25	2.00	17.50
4 to 5 ft., well-branched, field-grown	.75	6.00	50.00
3 to 4 ft., well-branched, field-grown	.50	4.00	35.00

Citrange

Citranges are products of Mr. Weber of the United States Department of Agriculture, Washington, D. C. They are crosses of the Citrus trifoliata and the best varieties of Oranges in cultivation. In these crosses Mr. Weber has made it possible to produce fairly palatable Oranges in sections of the country where the mercury goes to zero. These Citranges have been tested for a number of years, and in this section it is seldom that the foliage is injured by the cold. The leaves are trifoliate but of large size; thus showing the blood of the Citrus trifoliata and the Orange.

We offer strong, grafted plants of several named varieties as follows: Morton, Rusk and Willet.

	Each	10
12 to 15 in., branched	$0.50	$4.00

Citrus Fruits

All of our Citrus fruits are grown upon Citrus trifoliata unless otherwise stated. Varieties budded on Citrus trifoliata bear at an early age, and the trees grow off rapidly and the plants are more resistant to cold.

AUGUSTA, GEORGIA.

CITRUS FRUITS—Continued.

Kumquat or Kinkan. We offer two varieties of this popular little citrus fruit—Marumi, round; Nagami, oblong. This plant is of dwarf, bushy growth, seldom exceeding a height of 10 to 12 feet, and is of compact and spreading habit. Fruit about the size of a small plum; rind sweet; juice acid. It is eaten whole. Also excellent for preserves and marmalade; exceedingly productive; an early bearer. Will stand in open ground in Augusta, but will give the best results if protected during exceedingly cold snaps.

	Each	10	100
24 to 30 in., very bushy	$1.50	$12.50	
18 to 24 in., very heavy, well branched	1.25	10.00	
15 to 18 in., 3 years, grafted, heavy, well branched	1.00	8.00	
12 to 15 in., 2 years, grafted, heavy, well branched	.75	5.00	
10 to 12 in., 2 years, grafted, well branched	.50	3.50	$30.00

Lemon. AMERICAN WONDER, OR PONDEROSA. (On own roots). We have a fine stock of well-branched, specimen plants, bearing size.

	Each	10
18 to 24 in., bushy	$0.75	$6.00
15 to 18 in., bushy	.50	4.00

Lemon. BELAIR, GENOA, LAMB'S and other best sorts.

	Each	10
30 to 36 in., very bushy	$2.00	
24 to 30 in., well branched	1.50	
18 to 24 in., well branched	1.00	
15 to 18 in., well branched	.75	
12 to 15 in., branched	.50	$4.00

Orange. (*Otaheite*). CHINESE DWARF ORANGE. (On own roots). Plants of bushy habit, beginning to bloom when less than one foot in height. Fruit small, of inferior quality, but produced in great profusion. A very desirable variety for pots.

	Each	10
18 to 24 in., bushy	$1.00	$7.50
15 to 18 in., well branched	.75	6.00

Satsuma, or Oonshiu. So far this is the hardiest known edible Orange. It is of the Mandarin type. At Augusta it has stood a temperature of 12° above zero without injury. The trees are of drooping habit with broad, spreading heads; thornless; bears early. The fruit is of medium size, flattened like the Mandarin; color deep orange, flesh tender and juicy; seedless; ripens at Augusta in September and October. All of our Satsumas are field-grown and grafted on Citrus trifoliata.

	Each	10	100
4-yrs., 4-5 ft., very bushy	$2.00	$15.00	
3-yrs., 3-4 ft., bushy	1.50	10.00	$80.00
2-3 ft., well-branched	1.00	7.50	60.00
18-24 in., branched	.75	6.00	40.00
12-18 in., branched	.50	4.00	30.00

Orange.—Washington Naval and other good sorts, grafted on Citrus Trifoliata.

	Each	10
18 to 24 in., well branched	$1.00	$7.50
15 to 18 in., well branched	.75	6.00
12 to 15 in., well branched	.50	4.00

Pomelo, or Grape Fruit. One of the most popular citrus fruits now grown. For the orange belt only.

	Each	10
30 to 36 in., well branched	$1.50	
24 to 30 in., well branched	1.00	$7.00
15 to 18 in., well branched	.75	6.00

Cleyera. Japanese Cleyera.

Cleyera Japonica. A shrub of medium height; foliage very glossy; flowers creamy white, produced in great profusion during June; delightfully fragrant; followed by red berries, which are retained all winter.

	Each	10
15 to 18 in., well branched, from 4 inch pots	$0.75	$6.00
12 to 15 in., strong, from 3 in. pots	.50	4.00

Cotoneaster

Cotoneaster Simonsi, or Nepalensis. Attains a height of about 4 feet; dark green leaves; flowers white, slightly pinkish, followed by bright red fruit. Blooms last of April. One of the best.

	Each	10	100
3 to 4 ft., extra heavy, bushy	$0.60	$5.00	
24 to 30 in., extra heavy, bushy	.50	4.00	$30.00
18 to 24 in., bushy	.25	2.25	20.00

Crataegus. Thorn.

Crataegus Lalandii. LALAND'S THA. PYRACANA a beautiful sub-variety of the evergreen burning bush. Very effective and desirable. In early spring the plant is covered with a profusion of white flowers, which are followed by bright orange berries, these being retained during the entire winter.

	Each	10
3 to 4 ft., extra heavy, well branched	$1.00	$8.00
2 to 3 ft., heavy, well branched	.75	6.00
18 to 24 in., well branched	.50	4.00

Elaeagnus. Japan Oleaster.

We cannot too highly recommend these beautiful shrubs, which are perfectly hardy here, do not require very rich soil, and are not affected by either extreme heat or cold. The variegated-foliaged varieties are exceedingly showy.
Prices except where noted:

	Each	10
18 to 24 in., heavy, grafted from pots	$1.00	
15 to 18 in., well branched, grafted from pots	.75	$6.00
12 to 15 in., branched, grafted from pots	.50	4.00

Elaeagnus aurea maculata.

Elaeagnus aurea maculata. GOLDEN-LEAVED OLEASTER. Foliage broad, beautifully blotched and striped golden yellow. Produces in March fruit the size of the cranberry, which, combined with the beautiful foliage, makes a most unique plant.

E. aurea variegata. Broad, dark green leaves, beautifully bordered and blotched light yellow.

E. macrophylla. Leaves very large, undulated, clear green on upper side, silvery white beneath. A showy and conspicuous shrub. Scarce.

E. Pungens. Leaves two to four inches long, very dark green above, silvery beneath, margin of leaf undulating; creamy white, fragrant flowers produced in January; a beautiful shrub.

	Each	10	100
18 to 24 inches, strong, well branched	$1.00	$8.00	
15 to 18 inches, well branched	.75	6.00	$50.00
12 to 15 inches, branched	.50	4.00	30.00

P. J. BERCKMANS CO.

ELAEAGNUS—Continued.

E. Simoni. SIMON'S OLEASTER. Foliage elongated, silvery on under side; of compact growth; has edible fruit. A most desirable plant for the lawn.

	Each	10
15 to 18 in., very strong, from open ground	$0.75	$6.00
12 to 15 in., well branched, from pots and from open ground	.50	4.00

ENGLISH LAUREL. See Laurocerasus

Eriobotrya. Loquat: Japan Medlar.

Eriobotrya Japonica, Seedlings. This plant is well adapted to the southern coastal belt. Trees of medium height, with long, glossy, evergreen leaves; fruit, bright-yellow, round or oblong, about the size of a Wild Goose Plum; borne in clusters from the end of February until May; seldom perfects fruit in this locality, but is very successful southward.

	Each	10	100
4 years	$0.50	$4.00	
3 years	.35	3.00	$25.00
2 years	.25	2.00	17.50

E. Giant. Fruit four times as large as the common Japanese Medlar seedling; very handsome foliage.

	Each	10
Strong, 2 year, grafted plants	$0.50	$4.00

Escallonia Montevidiensis.

Escallonia Montevidiensis, or floribunda. A profuse blooming shrub, attaining a height of 10 to 15 feet. Leaves bright, shining green; white flowers in umbels, produced during June and July. Very scarce and desirable.

	Each	10
Extra strong, from 4 in. pots	$0.75	$6.00
Strong, from 3 in. pots	.50	4.00

Gardenia.

Gardenia. Cape Jasmine.

Very popular evergreen shrubs with bright, glossy foliage. Hardy as far north as Virginia and Tennessee. They do well in almost any well-drained soil. Large, fragrant white flowers are freely produced from middle of May until fall.

Prices except where noted:

	Each	10	100
18 to 24 inches, well branched, from pots	$0.75	$6.00	
15 to 18 inches, well branched, from pots	.50	4.00	$30.00
12 to 15 inches, from pots	.25	2.00	17.50

Gardenia florida. Flowers very large, white, and very fragrant; foliage glossy; blooms middle of May.

G. Fortunei. Flowers larger than those of G. florida.

G. radicans. DWARF CAPE JASMINE. A very dwarf, trailing Cape Jasmine; foliage very small; flowers white, very fragrant. Most desirable where a low effect is desired.

	Each	10	100
8 to 12 in., bushy, from 4 inch pots	$0.50	$4.00	
6 to 8 in., well branched, from 3 inch pots	.25	2.00	$17.50

Ilex. Holly.

Ilex aquifolium. ENGLISH OR EUROPEAN HOLLY. Leaves of intense, deep, shining green, with undulating, spine-tipped margins. Berries bright scarlet, which, combined with the glossy green leaves, makes this a conspicuous plant for winter effect.

	Each	10
15 to 18 in., very strong	$0.75	
12 to 15 in., strong	.50	$4.00

I. Opaca. AMERICAN HOLLY. In transplanting, the plants should be defoliated and the large sizes should also be severely pruned.

	Each	10	100
4 to 5 ft., heavy, well branched, transplanted, from open ground	$2.50		
3 to 4 ft., heavy, well branched, transplanted, from open ground	2.00		
2 to 3 ft., branched, transplanted	1.50		
18 to 24 inches, branched, transplanted	1.00	$7.50	
15 to 18 inches, from pots	.50	4.00	$35.00
12 to 15 inches, from pots	.35	3.00	25.00

Escallonia.

ILEX—Holly—Continued.

I. Vomitoria. (*I. Cassine*). CASSENA OR YAUPON. A native shrub with spreading branches and small oval or oblong leaves. Sometimes attains a height of 25 feet. During the winter the plant is a mass of scarlet berries which makes it most conspicuous. Very effective when planted in groups; also makes an effective hedge.

	Each	10	100
18 to 24 inches, well branched, from pots	$0.50	$4.00	$30.00
12 to 18 inches, from pots	.25	2.00	17.50

Illicium. Anise.

Illicium anisatum. (*I. religiosum*). EAST INDIA. ANISE TREE. A handsome evergreen with broad, light-green leaves, which, when bruised, emit an anise fragrance. Attains a height of 10 to 20 feet. Very desirable.

	Each	10
2 to 3 ft., well branched	$0.75	$6.00
18 to 24 in., branched	.50	4.00
15 to 18 in.	.35	3.00

Kalmia. American Laurel.

Kalmia latifolia. CALICO BUSH. A beautiful native, broad-leaved evergreen shrub, often attaining the size of a small tree. Its thick, waxy leaves are retained the year round, giving a striking effect. The pink and white geometrically-shaped buds appear and expand into beautiful white and flesh-colored flower cups. Of greatest value for massing, making a beautiful effect in the landscape.

	Each	10	100
18 to 24 in., extra strong clumps, from open ground	$2.00	$17.50	
12 to 18 in., extra strong clumps, from open ground	1.25	10.00	
18 to 24 in., bushy, from open ground	1.00	8.00	
12 to 18 in., bushy, from open ground	.50	4.00	$30.00

Kalmia.

Laurocerasus. English or Cherry Laurel.

These are valuable shrubs. Their principal merits are great vigor; beautiful, broad shining foliage; of easy cultivation, and thrive in any ordinary, good, well-drained garden soil. Not hardy north of Washington, D. C. They attain a hight from 12 to 15 feet with a corresponding breadth. The plants do not bloom until they are several years old, when they produce spikes of small, white flowers. For massing or for single specimens few plants possess more advantages than the English Laurel.

	Each	10	100
3 to 3½ ft. very bushy	$2.00		
30 to 36 in., very bushy	1.50	$12.50	
24 to 30 in., well branched	1.25	10.00	$80.00
18 to 24 in., well branched	1.00	8.00	70.00
15 to 18 in., well branched	.75	6.00	50.00
12 to 15 in., well branched	.50	4.00	35.00

Laurocerasus Bertini. Foliage very broad; dark green.
L. Caucasica. Foliage broad, light green. A fine sort.

English Laurel.

L. Colchica. Dark foliage, which is gray-green beneath.
L. rotundifolia viridis. Leaves short, broad, light green.
L. Triumph of Bordeaux. A new variety, with broad, dark foliage; medium grower.
L. Triumph of Boskoop. New; foliage broad, dark green. A very desirable, tall-growing variety.
L. Versaillensis. Broad foliage. Quite distinct.

Laurus. Laurel; Bay Tree.

This beautiful evergreen is very popular, and is perfectly hardy in the middle South and southward. The tree will attain a height of 30 feet. This Laurel is a tree which is commonly grown in standard or pyramidal shape and used as a tub plant, but the plants we offer are not trimmed in standard or pyramidal shape, but are grown in bush form.

	Each	10	100
18 to 24 inches, strong, well branched, from pots	$1.00	$8.00	
15 to 18 inches, well branched from pots	.75	6.00	$50.00
12 to 15 inches, branched, from pots	.50	4.00	35.00

Laurus nobilis. SPICE, OR APOLLO'S LAUREL. A beautiful evergreen, with long, narrow, glossy green leaves, which are very aromatic, and are used in cooking.
L. regalis. A variety of Spice, or Apollo's Laurel. Leaves beautifully crimped. A distinct variety.

LAURUSTINUS. See Viburnum Tinus

Ligustrum. Privet.

None of our broad-leaved evergreens give a greater form of foliage and growth than Ligustrums. For groups or individual specimens there is nothing more desirable.

Ligustrum Amurense. AMOOR RIVER PRIVET. True. From Amoor River. Very rapid and compact grower; foliage small. No finer hedge plant is grown. (See under head of Hedge Plants). It is also desirable for single specimens or for wind-breaks. For these, plant 8 to 10 feet apart.

	Each	10	100
3 to 4 ft., strong, bushy	$0.25	$2.00	$15.00

L. Excelsum superbum. SILVER LEAVED PRIVET. A tall-growing form of Japanese Privet. Leaves large, beautifully variegated white and green. Stands sun to perfection; in winter the dark-purple berries are very effective. Ultimate height 12 to 15 ft.

P. J. BERCKMANS CO.

Ligustrum Japonicum.

LIGUSTRUM. PRIVET—Continued.

	Each	10	100
3 to 4 ft., grafted, very bushy	$1.00	$8.00	
2 to 3 ft., grafted, well branched		.75	6.00	$50.00
18 to 24 inches, grafted, well branched		.50	4.00	$37.50

L. Japonicum. JAPANESE PRIVET. A beautiful, broad-leaved variety. Foliage dark green, with panicles of white flowers, followed by purple berries. Can be grown into a small tree and trimmed in pyramidal standard or other forms. Ultimate height, 20 to 30 feet.

	Each	10	100
6 to 7 ft., extra heavy, bushy	$5.00		
5 to 6 ft., extra heavy, bushy	3.00	$25.00	
4 to 5 ft., extra heavy, bushy	2.00	17.50	
3 to 4 ft., heavy, well branched	1.00	9.00	$80.00
2 to 3 ft., well branched	.75	6.00	50.00
18 to 24 in., well branched	.50	4.00	37.50
15 to 18 in., well branched	.40	3.50	30.00

L. Japonicum, Standards. STANDARD JAPANESE PRIVET. These trees have trained heads similar to the Standard Bay trees, and where a cheap and hardy substitute for the Bay is desired, for either tubs or open ground, the above mentioned standard Privet is most desirable, as the plant is perfectly hardy in the South. All of these plants are from open ground, but have been several times transplanted, and will be lifted with a large ball of earth about the roots and same wrapped in burlaps.

	Each
Trees with 36 to 40-in. stems, 24 to 26-in. heads	$3.50
Trees with 36 to 40-in. stems, 18 to 20-in. heads	2.50

L. lucidum. A beautiful form of Japanese Privet. Leaves large, thick, ovate, lanceolate, of a very dark, shining green. Large heads of white flowers produced in May, followed by black berries, which are retained throughout the winter. Hardy at Baltimore. A most desirable variety. Attains a height of 20 feet.

	Each	10	100
3 to 4 feet, very bushy	$2.00		
30 to 36 inch, very bushy	1.50	$12.50	$100.00
24 to 30 in., very bushy	1.00	8.00	70.00
18 to 24 inch, very bushy	.75	6.00	50.00
15 to 18 inch, well branched	.50	4.00	35.00

L. macrophyllum. An exceedingly rare and beautiful form of the Japanese Privet. Leaves of immense size and of intense dark green color. A most distinct and attractive variety. Ultimate height, 12 to 15 feet.

PRICES:

	Each	10
18 to 24 inch, bushy, grafted	$1.00	
15 to 18 inch, very strong, grafted	.75	$6.00
12 to 15 inch, strong, grafted	.50	4.00

L. Marginatum aureum. GOLDEN LEAVED PRIVET. A vigorous growing variety with large leaves beautifully margined with yellow. Stands the sun well. In winter the large bunches of purple berries combined with the yellow foliage makes a very striking effect. Ultimate height 15 to 20 feet.

	Each	10	100
4 to 5 ft. grafted, very bushy specimens	$1.50	$12.50	
3 to 4 ft. grafted, very bushy specimens	1.00	8.00	$70.00
2 to 3 ft. grafted, well branched	.75	6.00	50.00
18 to 24 inches, grafted, branched	.50	4.00	37.50

L. Nepalense. NEPAUL PRIVET. Resembles the Japanese Privet, but of smaller and more compact growth, and leaves somewhat smaller. A desirable variety in every respect. Ultimate height, 10 to 15 feet.

	Each	10	100
3 to 4 feet, very bushy	$2.00		
30 to 36 inch, very bushy	1.50	$12.50	$100.00
24 to 30 in., very bushy	1.00	8.00	70.00
18 to 24 inch, very bushy	.75	6.00	50.00
15 to 18 inch, well branched	.50	4.00	35.00

L. ovalifolium. CALIFORNIA PRIVET. Growth erect; leaves larger than L. Amurense, but not equal to it as a hedge plant. It is grown North and West in large quantities.

	Each	10	100	1000
4 to 5 ft., very bushy, 4 years	$0.50	$4.00		
3 to 4 ft., bushy, 3 years	.25	2.00	$15.00	$100.00

Magnolia

Magnolia fuscata. (*Michelia fuscata*). BANANA SHRUB. A most popular and desirable evergreen shrub. Hardy South, but for conservatories in the colder sections. Yellowish white flowers, edged with maroon, appear in great profusion in early spring. The

Ligustrum Macrophyllum.

44

AUGUSTA, GEORGIA.

Magnolia grandiflora.

MAGNOLIA—Continued.

banana-like fragrance is so strong that it is recognizable several yards from the plant.

	Each	10	100
24 to 30 in., very bushy, from open ground	$2.00	$15.00	
24 to 30 in., well branched from pots	1.50	12.50	
18 to 24 in., well branched from pots	1.00	8.00	
15 to 18 in., well branched, from pots	.75	6.00	$50.00
12 to 15 in., branched from pots	.50	4.00	35.00
10 to 12 in., from pots	.35	3.00	25.00

Magnolia grandiflora. SOUTHERN MAGNOLIA. This is the grandest of all our native broad-leaved evergreen trees. It is a native of the middle sections of the southern states, and succeeds best in a rich soil. Nothing more conspicuous can be seen amongst evergreens when its large, white flowers are fully expanded. Their period of blooming begins the middle of April and lasts until August. Hardy at Philadelphia.

	Each	10	100
4 to 5 ft., well branched, from open ground	$1.00		
3 to 4 ft., well branched, from open ground	.75	$6.00	
2 to 3 ft., from open ground	.50	4.00	$30.00
2 to 3 ft., strong plants, from pots	.75	6.00	
15 to 20 in., from pots	.50	4.00	30.00
12 to 15 in., from pots	.40	3.00	25.00

Note—To lessen liability of loss from transplanting, leaves will be cut off from open-ground-grown plants, unless we are instructed to the contrary. Our Magnolias have been twice transplanted, and, therefore have finely-branched roots.

M. grandiflora gloriosa. LARGE FLOWERED MAGNOLIA. A variety of Grandiflora, with flowers of immense size, often 12 to 15 inches in diameter; foliage large, bronze underneath; a magnificent tree; very scarce.

	Each	10
18 to 24 in., grafted, heavy, pot-grown	$1.00	$9.00
15 to 18 in., grafted, heavy, pot-grown	.75	6.00
12 to 15 in., grafted, pot-grown	.50	4.00

Mahonia. Berberis.

Mahonia aquifolia. HOLLY-LEAVED ASHBERRY. A beautiful, hardy, low-growing, evergreen shrub, with prickly leaves; produces a profusion of yellow flowers in March. In winter the foliage assumes a bronze or copper color.

	Each	10
18 to 24 in.	$0.35	$3.00
12 to 18 in.	.25	2.00

Metrosideros. Bottle Brush.

Metrosideros Floribunda. (*Callistemon lanceolata*). A beautiful shrub with narrow, lanceolate leaves, reddish-brown when young. Bright red flowers produced in long, cylindrical spikes. Hardy at Savannah and southward. Ultimate height, 15 ft.

	Each	10
From 6 inch pots	$1.50	
From 5 inch pots	1.00	$8.00
From 4 inch pots	.50	4.00
From 3 inch pots	.40	3.00

Myrtus. Myrtle.

Myrtus communis. TRUE MYRTLE. A dwarf shrub, with small, bright green leaves; flowers pure white, very fragrant. Hardy at Augusta. Ultimate height, 10 feet.

	Each	10
15 to 18 in., very bushy	$0.75	
12 to 15 in., well branched	.50	$4.00

Nandina

Nandina domestica. JAPANESE NANDINA. A beautiful upright-growing shrub, with numerous reed-like stems springing from the same root. Leaves deep, glossy green, when young tinged with red. In winter beautiful coppery tones are assumed; white flowers produced in long panicles, followed by masses of small, bright red berries, which are retained all winter. Hardy at Washington, D. C. Ultimate height, 10 feet.

	Each	10	100
Strong plants from 4 in. pots	$0.50	$4.00	
Strong plants from 3 in. pots	.35	3.00	$25.00

Nerium. Oleander.

Neriums are all hardy in this latitude They have also been successfully grown along the coast in Southern New Jersey, but should be protected during winter.

	Each	10	100
3 to 3½ ft., well branched, from 5 inch pots	$1.00	$8.00	
20 to 30 in., well branched from 4 inch pots	.75	6.00	
15 to 20 in., from 4 in. pots	.50	4.00	$30.00
12 to 15 in., from 3 in. pots	.25	2.00	17.50

Mme. Peyre. Pale flesh; double corolla.
Professor Parlatorre. Pink; double corolla.
Single White. Heavy grower; continuous bloomer.

White Oleander.

45

P. J. BERCKMANS CO.

Olea

Olea fragrans. TEA, OR SWEET OLIVE. Small, white flowers, produced in clusters, which emit a pleasing fragrance. As a conservatory shrub for northern florists it will be found invaluable. The blooming period begins in the fall and lasts for several months. It is of easy culture.

	Each	10	100
18 to 24 in., well branched, from pots	$1.00	$8.00	
15 to 18 in., well branched, pot. grown	.75	6.00	
12 to 15 in., well branched, pot. grown	.50	4.00	$37.50
10 to 12 in., pot-grown	.35	3.00	25.00
8 to 10 in., pot-grown	.25	2.50	20.00

Osmanthus

Osmanthus aquifolium, or Olea illicifolia. HOLLY-LEAVED TEA OLIVE. A most beautiful evergreen shrub, with dark green, spiny-toothed leaves, resembling the Holly. In the fall and sometimes in the spring it produces deliciously fragrant white flowers in great profusion. This is one of the most desirable of the Broad-leaved Evergreens, and is just beginning to be appreciated. Tree attains a height of 25 to 30 feet. Hardy at New York.

	Each	10	100
2 to 3 ft., very bushy	$1.25	$10.00	
18 to 24 in., very bushy, pot. grown and open ground	1.00	8.00	
15 to 18 in., very bushy, pot grown	.75	6.00	$50.00
12 to 15 in., pot-grown, well branched	.50	4.00	35.00
10 to 12 in., pot-grown branched	.35	3.00	25.00

Phoenix. Date Palm.

Phoenix Canariensis. CANARY ISLAND DATE PALM. A very graceful and handsome Palm. Leaves pinnate and of a very deep dark green color. Makes a most effective plant on the lawn. Strong, vigorous grower; hardy at Charleston and southward.

	Each	10
15 to 18 in., strong, from 5 in. pots	$0.50	$4.00

Photinia

Photinia serrulata. EVERGREEN PHOTINIA. A large evergreen shrub, or small tree, the foliage of which becomes very conspicuous in fall, when it assumes a red shade. Flowers white, in large corymbs, produced in early spring. Strong plants from open ground. Plants will be defoliated before forwarding.

3 to 3½ ft., very heavy, budded	$1.00	
2 to 3 ft., heavy, budded	.75	$6.00
18 to 24 in., budded	.50	4.00

Pittosporum

Pittosporum Tobira. JAPANESE PITTOSPORUM. A fine shrub, with dark green leaves clustered at the ends of the branches. Plant is of compact growth; flowers yellowish white, very fragrant, produced the middle of April and last a long time. A splendid shrub for specimens or massing, and can also be trimmed in fanciful shapes.

	Each	10
15 to 18 in., well branched, from open ground	$0.75	$6.00
12 to 15 in., well branched, from open ground	.50	4.00

P. Tobira variegata. VARIEGATED PITTOSPORUM. Similar to P. Tobira, but with leaves beautifully margined white. Of dwarf habit.

	Each	10
12 to 15 in., very bushy, from open ground	$0.75	$6.00
10 to 12 in., well branched, from open ground	.50	4.00

PRIVET. See Ligustrum

Quercus acuta Japanese Evergreen Oak.

Quercus. The Oak.

Quercus acuta. JAPANESE EVERGREEN OAK. Without doubt this is the most beautiful evergreen Oak ever introduced. The tree is of medium growth; bark very smooth; leaves oblong, of a bright, glossy green; growth very symmetrical and compact. A specimen of this Oak in our grounds is the admiration of all who see it. Seems to do well in almost any soil; needs comparatively little care, but will repay any attention given.

	Each	10	100
15 to 18 in., pot grown	$0.35	$3.00	$25.00
12 to 15 in., pot grown	.25	2.25	20.00

Q. Darlington. DARLINGTON OAK. This is a very handsome form of Evergreen, or Live Oak. The tree is of more upright growth than the Live Oak. A magnificent species, and very popular wherever known.

	Each	10	100
12-14 ft. specimens, 2½ to 3½ in. cal	$6.00		
10-12 ft., 1½ to 2 in. cal	2.00		
8-10 ft., 1¼ to 1½ in. cal	1.00	$9.00	
6-8 ft., 1 to 1¼ in. cal	.75	6.00	$50.00
5-6 ft., in.	.50	4.00	35.00

Q. sempervirens. LIVE OAK. The native Live Oak of the South. We have a beautiful lot of stocky, transplanted trees.

	Each	10
8-10 ft., specimens, 1½ to 1¾ in. cal.	$1.50	
6-8 ft., 1¼ to 1½ in. cal	1.25	$10.00
5-6 ft., well branched	.75	6.00
4-5 ft.	.50	4.00
3-4 ft.	.40	3.00

All Oaks are very difficult to transplant; hence the trees must be defoliated and severely pruned when planted. Keep the trees well mulched until thoroughly established.

AUGUSTA, GEORGIA.

Rhododendron Ponticum at Fruitlands.

Raphiolepsis Indica. Indian Hawthorn.

Raphiolepsis Indica. (*Crataegus Indica*). INDIAN HAWTHORN. A dwarf-growing shrub with spreading branches; leave ovate, very dark green. White flowers produced in loose panicles in early spring, followed by black berries which are retained for a long time. Exceedingly rare.

	Each.
Strong plants, 15 to 18 in., from pots	$1.00
Strong plants, 10 to 12 in., from pots	.50

Rhododendron

Rose Bay; Mountain Laurel

Rhododendron Catawbiense. CATAWBA RHODODENDRON. This is our native variety from the Alleghany Mountains, and those who have visited these mountains can appreciate this grand plant. Flowers lilac-purple.

	Each	10
12 to 18 in., branched	$1.00	$8.00

R. Catawbiense, Hardy Hybrids. These magnificent plants cannot be too highly recommended for those sections where they will give good results. They are indispensable in the landscape. To secure the most pleasing effect, they should be planted in large groups, as the rich and glowing colors of the flowers are most effective when viewed against a background of green formed by the glossy foliage of the plants. Then, too, when the flowers have faded, the plants themselves make a green shrub border that is unusually attractive. The varieties vary in color from pure white to deep purple and all shades of rose, pink and crimson. The plants should be set in a rich, shady situation, and the soil should contain well-decayed leaf-mold and peat. Keep the plants well mulched with rotted leaves. Not being deeply rooted, they are apt to be injured by drought.

	Each	10
18 to 24 in., branched, well set with buds	$2.00	$15.00
12 to 15 in., branched, well set with buds	1.25	10.00

R. maximum. GREAT LAUREL. Native of the Alleghany Mountains. Produces large trusses of pure white flowers. Blooms later than R. Catawbiense.

	Each	10
1½ to 2 ft., branched	$1.50	
1 to 1½ ft., branched	1.00	$8.00

R. ponticum. Asiatic species. These beautiful shrubs are perfectly hardy here, but require a shady situation and a soil rich in leaf-mold. Produces purple blooms last of April. Never plant where exposed all day to direct sunshine.

	Each	.10
20 to 24 in., well branched, well set with buds	$1.25	$10.00
15 to 18 in., well branched, well set with buds	1.00	7.50

TEA OLIVE. See Olea fragrans.

Thea. Tea Plant.

Thea Bohea. (*Camellia Thea*). CHINESE TEA PLANT. The true Assam Tea Plant, the leaves of which are used in making the different grades of tea of commerce. This is a very desirable medium-growing, broad-leaved evergreen. The plant attains a height from 10 to 15 feet. This beautiful shrub produces during November and December large white flowers with woolly anthers which resemble a single Camellia.

	Each	10	100
15-18 in., branched, from pots	$0.50	$4.00	$35.00
12 to 15 in., strong, from pots	.35	3.00	25.00

Viburnum

Viburnum odoratissimum. A Japanese variety with broad, glossy green leaves; of spreading growth. Attains a height of 10 feet. Very fragrant, pure white flowers in large panicles produced about the middle of April. A very handsome shrub.

	Each	10	100
18 to 24 in., from pots and open ground	$1.00	$8.00	$70.00
15 to 18 in., from pots and open ground	.50	4.00	35.00
12 to 15 in., from pots	.40	3.00	

V. Suspensum. (*V. Sandankwa*). From the Loochoo Islands. A shrub of compact, rapid growth, attaining a height of 6 to 8 ft. Leaves dark-green, paler beneath. Flowers creamy-white, resembling the Trailing Arbutus; blooms in February or March, followed by red fruit. Does best when protected from the afternoon sun of summer.

	Each	10
15 to 18 in, heavy, well branched, from pots	$0.75	$6.00
12 to 15 in., from pots	.50	4.00
10 to 12 in., from pots	.35	3.00

V. tinus. LAURUSTINUS. One of the handsomest and most satisfactory broad-leaved flowering shrubs; of rapid growth; attains a height of 10 feet. The flowers are creamy white, produced in the greatest profusion in early February, and last for a long time; very fragrant. The buds, before opening, are of a bright red.

	Each	10	100
24 to 30 in., strong plants from open ground	$1.50		
20 to 24 in., strong plants, from open ground	1.00	$8.00	
15 to 20 in., branched, from pots	.75	6.00	
12 to 15 in., branched, from pots	.50	4.00	$30.00
8 to 12 in., from pots	.35	3.00	25.00

Viburnum suspensum.

47

Yucca

Yucca aloifolia. SPANISH BAYONET, OR DAGGER. The well-known native variety. Leaves very stiff. dagger-shaped; flowers creamy white.

	Each	10	100
5 years, strong, transplanted	$0.50	$4.00	$30.00
4 years, strong, transplanted	.40	3.00	20.00
3 years, strong, transplanted	.25	2.00	17.50

Y. filamentosa. ADAM'S NEEDLE, OR BEAR GRASS. A conspicuous plant with stiff evergreen foliage. The large clusters of creamy white flowers produced in summer make a fine effect. Excellent for massing.

	Each	10	100
5 years, strong, transplanted	$0.50	$4.00	$30.00
4 years, strong	.40	3.00	20.00
3 years, strong	.25	2.00	15.00

Viburnum tinus.

Climbers and Trailers.

Climbing plants are indispensable for many ornamental uses, and are decidedly useful in nearly all of our garden operations. Some varieties are especially desirable for the beauty of their flowers; others for attractive foliage. They are easily cultivated, but must have proper care and attention in the matter of training. Possibly no Climbers offer greater possibilities as ornaments than Clematis Paniculata. Rhynchospermum and Wistaria, while Bignonias, Climbing Roses and Elaeagnus Reflexa are very useful for trellised hedges. Our Climbers are carefully grown and properly pruned, and are unusually vigorous. Nearly all in the list are hardy in the North.

Prices for special collection, 10 strong plants, in 10 varieties, our selection, $2.00; $15.00 per 100.

Akebia.

Akebia lobata. A JAPANESE CLIMBER. Very heavy foliage; purple flowers in long racemes. Produces a fruit that is quite popular in Japan. A very desirable Climber.

	Each	10
2 years, strong	$0.25	$2.00

A. quinata. A very popular ornamental Japanese Climber with beautiful foliage, almost evergreen. Peculiarly shaped, purple flowers produced in March.

	Each	10
2-year, strong	$0.25	$2.00

Allamanda

Allamanda Hendersonii. A beautiful Climber; almost perpetual bloomer. Yellow flowers of immense size. Not hardy here. Desirable only for sub-tropical sections. In colder localities it is largely used as a greenhouse climber.

	Each	10
Strong plants, from 3-in. pots	$0.30	$2.50

Ampelopsis. Ivy.

Ampelopsis Quinquefolia. VIRGINIA CREEPER. A deciduous native climber of rapid growth. Very hardy.

Banksia Rose.

AUGUSTA, GEORGIA.

AMPELOPSIS—Continued.

Leaves divided into five deeply cut leaflets which turn to rich crimson in the autumn. Desirable for covering trees, walls, banks and rocks.

	Each	10	100
3 years, extra strong field-grown	$0.25	$2.00	$15.00
2 years, strong, field-grown	.15	1.25	10.00

A. Veitchii. (*A. Japonica or Tricuspidata*). JAPANESE OR BOSTON IVY. A deciduous vine of rapid growth; suitable for covering walls, stumps, etc.

	Each	10	100
Strong, 3 year, from 4 in. pots, and open ground	$0.25	$2.25	$20.00
Strong, from 3 in. pots	.15	1.25	10.00

Antigonon Leptopus. Mexican Rose.

Antigonon leptopus. (*Rosa de Montana*). A beautiful climbing plant with tuberous roots; blooms freely from June until fall. Beautiful, rosy-pink flowers produced in large racemes. Leaves heart-shaped. A most desirable vine for the South. In this section tops die down in winter; it is, therefore, advisable to protect the roots with a mulching of leaves.

	Each	10
2 years, strong	$0.25	$2.00

Bignonia. Trumpet Vine.

Bignonia capreolata. (*Bignonia crucigera*). CROSS VINE. A very handsome, vigorous-growing native climber. In early April it produces in great profusion trumpet-shaped flowers about 2 inches long, reddish purple on outside, with yellow throat. Evergreen.

	Each	10	100
3 year, strong clumps, from open ground	$0.35	$3.00	$25.00
2 year, strong plants, from pots	.25	2.00	17.50

B. Hybrida. A handsome deciduous variety with dark, blood-red flowers; free bloomer. Hardy as far north as Boston, Mass.

	Each	10	100
3 years, extra heavy, grafted	$0.50	$4.00	
2 years, heavy, grafted	.35	3.00	
1 year, heavy, grafted	.25	2.25	$20.00

B. Grandiflora. JAPANESE TRUMPET VINE. A very desirable deciduous variety of medium growth. Can be kept trimmed as a bush, in which form it is very effective. Flowers very large, deep orange; commences to bloom in May and continues nearly the entire summer. Very desirable.

	Each	10
1 yr., grafted	$0.35	$3.00

Bignonia grandiflora.

B. Mme. Gallen. A desirable new variety, with dark, blood-red flowers with orange throat. In size the flower is between that of Bignonia hybrida and grandiflora. A very handsome and desirable hardy variety.

	Each	10
2 yrs., heavy, grafted	$0.50	$4.00
1 yr.		.35	3.00

B. venusta. (*Pyrostegia venusta*). FLAME FLOWER. A beautiful tropical variety of the Trumpet Vine. A rapid grower. Produces a great abundance of rich, orange-colored flowers. A conservatory plant of this section, but most desirable for sub-tropical sections.

	Each	10
2 year, from 3 inch pots	$0.25	$2.00

Clematis.

Clematis paniculata. JAPANESE CLEMATIS. Flowers white, star-shaped, produced during midsummer and fall upon long shoots. In addition to its profusion of fragrant flowers, the foliage is handsome.

	Each	10	100
3 yr., extra strong, field-grown	$0.50	$4.00	
2 yr., strong, field-grown	.25	2.00	$15.00

HYBRID CLEMATIS, LARGE-FLOWERING

	Each	10
Extra strong, field-grown	$0.60	$5.00
Strong, field-grown	.50	4.00

Clematis Henryi. Large; creamy white; free grower and bloomer. The finest white Clematis.

C. Jackmani. Large and intense violet-purple; free and abundant bloomer. This is the best and most popular of the large flowering Clematis.

C. Mme. Edouard Andre. Large; violet-red; strong grower and free bloomer.

Note—Clematis do best in a deep, rich, loamy soil, and should be frequently enriched. As soon as the plants are set out, they must be securely tied to canes or other supports.

Elaeagnus

Elaeagnus reflexa. CLIMBING ELAEAGNUS. A wonderfully vigorous Japanese evergreen climber. Leaves green above, silvery beneath, overspread with yellowish, light brown scales, giving the entire surface a bronze tint. The bark of the young growth is brown. This vine will go to the top of the highest tree, and, by frequent pruning, can be grown as a shrub.

	Each	10	100
2 to 3 ft., well-branched from pots and open ground	$0.50	$4.00	$35.00
18 to 24 in., strong, from pots and open ground	.35	2.50	20.00

Euonymus

Eponymus rudicans. CLIMBING EUONYMUS. A low, trailing evergreen of rapid growth. Fine for covering walls and stumps; good ground-covering for shady places.

	Each	10	100
15 to 18 in., extra strong, field-grown clumps	$0.35	$3.00	$25.00
12 to 15 in., field-grown clumps	.25	2.00	15.00
8 to 10 in., field-grown, or nice 6 to 8 in. plants, from 3-inch pots	.20	1.50	10.00

E. radicans variegata. VARIEGATED CLIMBING EUONYMUS. A beautiful evergreen creeping plant with very pretty foliage, which is beautifully variegated deep green and white. Very showy for covering low walls and stumps; it is also excellent for bordering, as it can be kept closely clipped.

	Each	10	100
15 to 18 in., extra strong field-grown clumps	$0.35	$3.00	
12 to 15 in., strong field-grown plants	.25	2.00	$15.00
8 to 10 in., field-grown, or 6 to 8 in. plants, from 3-in. pots	.20	1.50	10.00

P. J. BERCKMANS CO.

Clematis paniculata.

Ficus

Ficus repens. CLIMBING FIG. An evergreen climber with small, bright green leaves. This is an excellent plant for covering walls, rock and rustic work in greenhouses. Makes a dense, dark green covering. In protected situations the vine is hardy in Augusta.

	Each	10	100
Extra strong, from 3-in. pots	$0.25	$2.00	$15.00
Strong, from 2½-in. pots	.15	1.25	10.00

Gelsemium. Yellow Jasmine.

Gelsemium sempervirens. CAROLINA YELLOW JASMINE. Our native variety, with bright yellow, fragrant flowers, which are so profusely produced in early spring.

	Each	10
Strong clumps, nursery-grown	$0.25	$2.00

G. sempervirens flore plena. DOUBLE YELLOW JASMINE. A very rare sub-variety of our native Yellow Jasmine, with double flowers, which are produced in great profusion in early spring and more sparingly in the fall. If grown in the conservatory, flowers are produced nearly all winter. Very scarce.

	Each
Strong clumps	$0.50

Hedera. Ivy.

Hedera Algeriensis. ALGERIAN IVY. A very fine variety, with pretty green leaves of immense size. A rapid grower. A most conspicuous plant; not quite so hardy as the English Ivy.

	Each	10	100
Extra strong, from 4-in. pots	$0.40	$3.00	
Strong plants, from 3-in. pots	.25	2.00	$15.00

H. Helix. ENGLISH IVY. Too well known to need description.

	Each	10	100
3 to 4 ft., very heavy, from 3-in. pots	$0.25	$2.00	$15.00
Strong, from 2½ and 3-in. pots	.15	1.25	10.00

H. Helix. ENGLISH IVY. We offer an unnamed form of English Ivy with small white ribbed leaves. This is very hardy and makes an excellent plant as a ground cover or for covering walls, etc., as it is a compact grower.

	Each	10	100
Extra strong plants, from 4-in. pots	$0.25	$2.00	$15.00
Strong plants, from 2½ to 3-in. pots	.15	1.25	10.00

HONEYSUCKLE. See Lonicera

JAPANESE or BOSTON IVY. See Ampelopsis

Jasminum. Jasmine.

Jasminum Primulinum. NEW CHINESE JASMINE. This new variety, recently introduced from China, is a desirable acquisition to our list of hardy evergreen climbers. Light yellow flowers are produced in early spring, and the plant continues to bloom for three months or more. In general appearance the flowers resemble those of Jasminum nudiflorum, but are considerably larger, sometimes being 2 inches in diameter. The foliage is rich, dark-green. In this locality the vine is an evergreen. It is not hardy north of Washington without protection. This plant should have a place in every garden. It does best when pruned and fertilized.

	Each	10
Extra strong, 2 to 3 ft.	$0.50	$4.00
Strong, 18 to 24 in.	.25	2.00

Kadsura

Kadsura Japonica. A very handsome Japanese climbing evergreen. Leaves 4 to 5 inches in length, dark green. The young growth of both the stems and leaves is red, giving the plant a bright appearance; flowers inconspicuous. In winter the clusters of small fruit, when ripe, make the plant very attractive.

	Each	10
Strong, from 4-in. pots	$0.50	4.00

Lonicera. Honeysuckle.

Prices of all varieties:

	Each	10	100
3 years, extra strong	$0.35	$3.00	$25.00
2 years, strong	.25	2.00	15.00

Lonicera Brownii. SCARLET TRUMPET HONEYSUCKLE A strong and rapid-growing evergreen variety with orange-scarlet flowers, which are produced in April. A decided improvement upon L. sempervirens (Woodbine), both as to foliage and bloom.

L. Chinensis. CHINESE HONEYSUCKLE. A showy variety, with purplish evergreen foliage, changing to greener shade at maturity. Flowers white, tinged with purple on outside

L. Heckrotti. HECKROTT'S HONEYSUCKLE. Flowers rose-colored on the outside; yellow in the center. A most excellent evergreen variety. Blooms continually from early spring until winter.

L. Japonica. (L. Halliana). JAPANESE HONEYSUCKLE. A very vigorous evergreen climber. White flowers changing to yellow, are borne in great profusion in summer and sparingly in the autumn. Naturalized in many sections of the country. Good for trellises and ground-covers.

Parthenocissus

Parthenocissus Henryana. (Vitis Henryii). A very graceful deciduous plant, admirably adapted for clothing trellises and pergolas. Leaves digitate, composed of five lanceolate leaflets with serrate margins, and measuring three inches in length. They are variegated along the midrib and principal veins with silvery white and rose. This variation is constant through the summer and is more pronounced in the autumn when the green gives place to rich tints of red. A very rapid and vigorous climber.

	Each	10	100
Strong, field-grown, or from 4-inch pots	$0.35	$3.00	
Strong, field-grown, or from 3-inch pots	.25	2.00	$17.50

Rhynchospermum. Star Jasmine.

Rhynchospermum jasminoides. (Trachelospermum jasminoides). MALAYAN OR AFRICAN JASMINE. The best evergreen climber for this section. A very beautiful, hardy and rapid-growing plant; producing in abundance from April until July fragrant star-shaped, white flowers. When in full bloom this plant is most conspicuous. Very effective where a thick screen is desired.

	Each	10	100
Extra strong, from 4-in. pots	$0.50	$4.00	
Strong, from 3½-in. pots	.35	3.00	$25.00
Strong, from 3-in. pots	.25	2.25	20.00

Roses, Climbing

Prices, our own selection of varieties:

	Each	10	100
1-year, on own roots, strong, field-grown	$0.25	$2.00	$17.50
1-year, budded on Manetti, strong, field-grown	.35	3.00	25.00
2-year, budded on Manetti, extra strong, field-grown	.50	3.50	30.00

Note.—For description of varieties see under Roses, pages 61 to 64.

50

AUGUSTA, GEORGIA.

Rhynchospermum jasminoides.

Solanum. Potato Vine.

Solanum jasminoides grandiflora. A very rapid-growing climber with dark green leaves; white, star-shaped flowers with yellow centers, produced in large clusters. Very desirable. Not hardy north of Augusta. This is an improvement upon the old variety.

	Each	10	100
Strong, from 3 in. pots.	$0.25	$2.00	$17.50

Vinca.

Vinca major. LARGER PERIWINKLE. An old and favorite plant, with large blue flowers, produced in early spring; leaves larger and a more vigorous grower than V. minor; excellent for vases, rock-work and bordering slopes.

Strong clumps, from open ground, 25 cents each; $1.50 for 10; $10.00 per 100; $60.00 per 1,000.

V. major variegata. VARIEGATED PERIWINKLE OR TRAILING MYRTLE. Same as the above, except that the leaves are beautifully variegated with silvery white; excellent for vases and window-boxes.

	Each	10	100
Extra strong, from 4 in. pots	$0.40	$3.00	
Strong, from 3 in. pots	.25	2.00	$17.50

V. minor. COMMON PERIWINKLE; RUNNING OR TRAILING MYRTLE. A well-known trailing plant. Flowers blue; leaves dark green, but smaller than V. major.

	Each	10	100	1000
Strong clumps, from open ground	$0.25	$1.50	$10.00	$60.00

Wistaria

All of our Wistarias are grown from free-flowering plants, and these must not be confused with the Wistarias which are grown from seed.

	Each	10	100
4 years, extra heavy, grafted	$1.00	$8.00	
3 years, heavy, grafted	.50	4.00	$35.00
2 years, grafted	.30	2.50	20.00

Wistaria Chinensis. CHINESE PURPLE WISTARIA. The well-known, single purple flowered variety; free bloomer.

W. Chinensis alba. CHINESE WHITE WISTARIA. White-flowering; a beautiful, graceful climber. Free bloomer.

W. Chinensis flore plena. DOUBLE PURPLE WISTARIA. Until the vine is three years old it is a shy bloomer, but afterwards it becomes floriferous.

W. frutescens magnifica. (On own roots). Flowers in large, drooping racemes, pale blue, with a yellow center; blooms about a month later than the Chinese varieties; also produces flowers during the summer. Vigorous.

W. multijuga. JAPANESE WISTARIA. Flowers about a week later than Wistaria Chinensis. A distinct and showy variety. Flowers, single, light purple, in loose racemes 1 to 3 feet long. Does not bloom freely until the vine is about 3 years old.

Wistaria.

Ornamental Hedge Plants.

Nothing can be more desirable for street protection or property divisions than a well-grown and carefully trimmed hedge. It may be a little more expensive than a fence in the beginning, but no repairs are required, and it grows in beauty from year to year.

For dividing lines, where a low hedge is desired, nothing is more appropriate than Abelia grandiflora, Berberis Thunbergii, Spiræa Thunbergii or Viburnum tinus. All of these plants are graceful in form and beautiful in foliage and flowers. For formal plantings the Amoor and California Privet, Boxwood and Carolina Cherry are unsurpassed. All are evergreen and easily cared for and make a dense and compact growth.

Note—Not less than 40 plants will be furnished at the price quoted per hundred; not less than 400 at the price quoted per thousand.

Abelia

Abelia grandiflora. (*A. rupestris*). This beautiful Broad-Leaved Evergreen is becoming a very popular hedge plant. As this makes a very bushy growth, the plants can be set 18 to 24 inches apart.

	100
12 to 18 inches, strong plants from open ground	$25.00

Berberis. Barberry.

Berberis Thunbergii. THUNBERG'S BARBERRY. A most beautiful dwarf Barberry from Japan. The bright green foliage changes to tones of red in autumn. The bright red berries in spring make a beautiful contrast with the green foliage. Leaves retained for a

Original Hedge of Amoor privet, Planted at Fruitlands in 1868 and Still in Fine Condition.

51

P. J. BERCKMANS CO.

BERBERIS THUNBERGII—Continued.

long time. Makes a most beautiful and conspicuous low-growing hedge, and one that is specially suited for making boundary lines.

	100
12 to .18 in., well branched	$15.00

Buxus. Boxwood.

Buxus Sempervirens. TREE BOX. Home-grown. This is a familiar variety found in many of the old-time gardens. It makes an admirable hedge plant, as it stands shearing well and can be kept at any height desired.

	100	1000
10 to 12 in., very bushy	$20.00	
8 to 10 in., very bushy	15.00	$125.00
6 to 8 in., bushy	8.00	60.00

B. suffruticosa. DWARF BOX. This is the variety so extensively used in the old-time gardens for edging walks and beds. It is of very slow growth, and its ultimate height is from 4 to 5 feet. The plants

Block of Boxwood.

should be set from 3 to 4 inches apart. We offer a superb lot of home-grown plants.

	100	1000
8 to 10 in., very bushy, 4 to 5 inches in diameter	$20.00	
6 to 8 in., very bushy, 3 to 4 inches in diameter	10.00	$80.00
4 to 6 in., bushy	8.00	60.00

Cerasus. Carolina Cherry.

Cerasus Caroliniana. (*Prunus Caroliniana*). MOCK ORANGE OF THE SOUTH.

	100	1000
12 to 18 in., well-branched	$17.50	
8 to 12 in., 1-year seedlings	$3.00	$15.00

Citrus trifoliata. Hardy Orange.

Citrus trifoliata. JAPAN HARDY ORANGE; TRIFOLIATE ORANGE. This popular plant was first disseminated by us, and is the coming hedge-plant for defensive as well as ornamental purposes. Far more desirable than Osage Orange. It is hardy as far north as New Jersey, and if planted in good soil an impenetrable hedge can be had three years from planting. In early spring, when covered with myriads of white flowers, nothing is more attractive; and while not an evergreen, the vivid green wood makes it appear bright during the winter. Plants may be set one foot apart. The plants require two or three annual shearings, the first about the middle of May and the others while the young growth is tender. If delayed until the wood is hardened, it will require more time and increased labor. An excellent hedge-knife can be made by taking a 28-inch scythe blade, straightening the shank and riveting it to a 14 or 18-inch straight wooden handle.

	100	1000
3 years, 3 to 4 ft., extra strong, well branched	$15.00	$100.00
3 years, 2 to 3 ft., strong, well branched	6.00	50.00
2 years, 18 to 24 in., well branched	4.00	30.00

Ligustrum. Privet.

Ligustrum Amurense. AMOOR RIVER PRIVET. The true variety. For the South it is far superior to the California Privet, which loses its leaves during winter,

Citrus Trifoliata Hedge.

whereas the Amoor River Privet retains its foliage throughout the entire year. Since 1866 we have cultivated and disseminated millions of the Amoor River Privet, and it is without doubt the most popular evergreen hedge plant of the day. It is of rapid growth, adapts itself to almost any soil not too arid or extremely wet. If properly treated, a hedge may be secured in two years after planting.

	100	1000
2 to 3 ft., well branched, transplanted	$5.00	$40.00

Note—To save freight, we always cut back Amoor River Privet before shipping, unless instructed to the contrary. This also avoids the possibility of the plants heating, should there be delay in transit.

L. ovalifolium. CALIFORNIA PRIVET. This is a very popular variety for hedges North and West. Leaves are larger and growth more erect than L. Amurense.

	100	1000
3 years, 3 to 4 ft., very bushy	$15.00	$100.00
2 years, 2 to 3 ft., well branched	4.00	30.00
18 to 24 in., branched	3.00	25.00

How to Make a Privet Hedge—Prepare the ground by plowing or spading to the proper width and depth. Open the trench 12 inches wide by 15 inches deep. Apply to this a liberal amount of well-rotted stable manure, and if this is not available, bone meal or some high grade of fertilizer. Mix the manure or fertilizer thoroughly with the soil. Set the plants in a straight line in the trench one foot apart, about one inch deeper than they originally stood in the nursery row. Firm the earth well about the roots, level off, and then cut the plants back to within four inches of the ground. In the spring, after the plants have made a growth of six or eight inches, cut off one-half of this growth, both side and top, and proceed in a like manner with each succeeding growth until your hedge has reached the desired height and width. Cultivate well.

Spiraea

Spiraea Thunbergii. THUNBERG'S SPIRAEA. Of dwarf habit; branches slender and drooping; foliage very narrow, light green, changing to bright orange and red in fall; flowers small, white, which appear very early in March and last three weeks. A beautiful variety for a dwarf or low-growing hedge.

	100
18 to 24 in., heavy, well branched	$15.00

Viburnum.

Viburnum tinus. LAURUSTINUS. This makes a very handsome and unique hedge, but care must be taken not to trim too severely; otherwise it will not bloom freely.

	100
12 to 15 in., branched, from pots	$30.00
8 to 12 in., from pots	25.00

Ornamental Grasses

ALL HARDY IN THIS LATITUDE

These are very effective as ornamental screens or for planting in masses or groups.

Arundo. Giant Reed.

Arundo donax variegata. VARIEGATED GIANT REED. A hardy, vigorous variety with long leaves, striped green and white, very striking.

	Each	10
Strong roots	$0.25	$2.00

Bambusa. Bamboo.

Bambusa aurea. (*Phyllistachys aurea*). GOLDEN BAMBOO. A graceful Japanese variety, with quantities of yellow stems from 15 to 20 feet. Leaves green and drooping; very numerous delicate branches. One of the hardiest Bamboos.

	Each	10
Extra strong	$1.00	
Strong	.50	$4.00

Eulalia Japonica

(Miscanthus Sinensis).

	Each	10	100
Extra large clumps, 18 in. diam.	$2.00	$17.50	
Large clumps, 12 in. diam.	1.00	8.00	
Strong clumps	.50	4.00	
Strong plants, from pots	.25	2.00	$15.00

Eulalia Japonica Gracillima. (*E. Univitatta*). A variety with narrow foliage and with a narrow stripe running through middle of leaf; very graceful.

E. Japonica variegata. STRIPED EULALIA. A variegated, hardy grass from Japan. In appearance it somewhat resembles the ribbon grass while in a young state. It forms compact clumps 6 feet in diameter. Its flower-stalks are graceful and numerous.

E. Japonica zebrina. ZEBRA-STRIPED EULALIA. Similar in habit to the above, but with its leaves blotched with gold. The stripe, instead of running longitudinally, like the former, runs across the leaf.

Gynerium. Pampas Grass.

	Each	10	100
Extra heavy clumps, 12 to 18 in. in diameter	$2.00		
Heavy clumps, 8 in. in diameter	1.00		
Strong clumps	.50		
Strong plants, from 3 and 4-in. pots	.25	$2.00	$15.00

Gynerium argenteum. WHITE PAMPAS GRASS. With silvery, plume-like spikes of flowers. An old favorite for grouping on the lawn.

G. Roi de Roses. PINK PAMPAS GRASS. Plumes very compact, of a delicate rose color. A very beautiful and scarce variety.

Coniferous Evergreens.

Evergreens are always in favor for landscape work, their deep green foliage making a strong background for the brilliant colors of summer; but it is in winter, when the northern landscape is barren of color and foliage, and the beauty of the southern greatly lessened, that they are most appreciated, the absence of other colors tending to bring out their beauty of form in a most striking manner.

It is an undisputed fact that at Fruitland Nurseries we grow the largest and most varied stock of coniferous evergreens in the southern states, and especially do we give attention to such varieties as are best adapted to this warmer climate. In our collection of Biotas, Cupressus, Retinosporas, Juniperus, etc., may be found many rare and valuable specimens. We also grow large quantities of the hardier varieties, adapted to the northern part of the country.

Our conifers are grown in the most careful and scientific manner. Nearly all of the open-ground plants have been grown one year in pots and then set in the open ground, and are afterwards several times transplanted. Therefore we can offer to our patrons plants with excellent root-systems. Many varieties of conifers are grown in the open ground during the summer, lifted in the early fall and potted, and, before being shipped, plants have already started new roots. All plants, both from open ground and pots, are shipped with a ball of earth around the roots, which is wrapped in burlap or moss.

Place the plant in the properly prepared hole; cut the string, so that the burlap can be released from about the ball of the plant, and plant in the same manner as instructions given under head of Broad-leaved Evergreens. Keep the plants well watered and mulched. The best seasons for transplanting are from November to December, and from February to March, but in the lower sections, where the ground does not remain frozen during the winter, planting can be successfully done any time when the ground is in proper condition. We have a superb lot of shapely specimen plants of many varieties of conifers. These are from ten to twenty years of age, and have been several times sheared and transplanted. Those desiring immediate effect will secure it by using the above-mentioned specimens. The prices vary from $5.00 to $100.00 each, according to size. See "Specimen Conifers," page 60.

P. J. BERCKMANS CO.

Field of Biota aurea conspicua.

PRICES OF SPECIAL COLLECTION OF CONIFERS

We will supply 10 fine plants, distinct varieties, our selection, 12 to 24 inches, for ....$ 4.00
Or 100 fine plants, in 25 or 30 varieties, our selection, for 30.00

Arbor-vitae. Biota and Thuya.

ASIATIC SECTION

Biota aurea conspicua. Originated by us; of compact, erect and symmetrical habit. Foliage intense gold; some of its branches being of a solid metallic tint, other suffused with green. As its name implies, it it most conspicuous; easily grown; and has stood perfectly in the east and west 20 degrees below zero. The original plant now stands in our grounds at Augusta, Georgia..

	Each	10	100
6 to 7 ft., beautiful, compact specimens	$6.00	$50.00	
5 to 6 ft., beautiful, compact specimens, 18 to 20 in. in diameter	4.00	35.00	
4 to 5 ft., beautiful, compact specimens	2.50	20.00	
3 to 4 ft., compact	2.00	15.00	
30 to 36 in., compact	1.00	8.00	
24 to 30 in., compact	.75	6.00	$50.00
18 to 24 in., compact	.50	4.00	35.00

B. aurea nana. BERCKMANS' GOLDEN ARBOR-VITAE. The ever-increasing demand for this, the most popular of all Biotas, shows the great popularity of this plant. Originated by us. It is of very dwarf, compact and symmetrical habit; a perfect gem for small gardens or cemetery lots. It far surpasses in every way its parent, the old Biota aurea. For window-boxes and vases this plant is most effective. It is desirable where it is too cold for palms and other decorative plants, For formal gardens it is a great favorite. In many sections it has stood a temperature of 10 degrees below zero without injury.

	Each	10	100
4 to 4½ ft., beautiful, compact specimens, 24 to 30 in. in diam. at base	$5.00		
40 to 44 in., beautiful, compact specimens, 24 in. in diam. at base	$4.00		
30 in., beautiful compact specimens	2.00	$17.50	
24 to 30 in., beautiful, compact specimens	1.50	12.50	$100.00
20 to 24 in., compact specimens	1.00	8.00	70.00
15 to 20 in., compact specimens	.75	6.00	50.00
12 to 15 in., compact specimens	.50	4.00	35.00

B. aurea pyramidalis. Originated by us. Of erect, symmetrical and compact growth. Of beautiful, golden tint. Its columnar habit adapts it to formal planting and suits it to lawn planting and evergreen groups. Will attain a height of 20 to 25 feet.

	Each	10
6 to 7 ft., beautiful, compact specimens.	$5.00	
5 to 6 ft., beautiful, compact specimens.	4.00	
24 to 30 in, compact specimens	.50	$4.00

B. Japonica filiformis. A Japanese variety with thread-like foliage; compact habit. We consider this one of the most distinct and desirable novelties, and it is becoming a great favorite. Well suited for cemeteries; also desirable for tubs. Will probably attain a height of 10 to 12 feet.

	Each	10	100
3 to 4 ft., beautiful, compact specimens	$3.00	$25.00	
30 to 36 in., beautiful, compact specimens	2.00	15.00	
24 to 30 in., very compact	1.00	8.00	$70.00
18 to 24 in., heavy	.75	6.00	50.00
15 to 18 in., heavy	.50	4.00	35.00

B. Pyramidalis. In this we have succeeded in getting a form of the pyramidal arbor-vitae which does not become brown during winter, but retains constantly

AUGUSTA, GEORGIA.

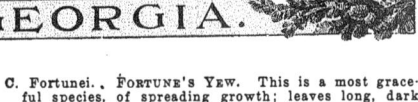

Biota Japonica filiformis.

BIOTA. ARBOR-VITAE—Continued.
its bright-green color; of compact and pyramidal habit. A plant which fills a long-felt want.

	Each	10
3 to 4 ft.	$2.00	$15.00
2 to 3 ft.	1.00	8.00
18 to 24 inches	.50	4.00

B. Rosedale. Originated in Texas. Foliage very fine, light green in summer, assuming a purplish hue in winter.

	Each
3½ to 4 ft., compact specimens	$2.00
36 to 40 in., compact specimens	1.50

Cedrus. Cedar.

Cedrus Atlantica. MOUNT ATLAS CEDAR. Similar to Cedrus Deodara, but foliage more compact and of a darker green. The tree attains large and stately proportions. Hardy in New York. Rapid grower and attains a height of 60 to 80 feet.

	Each	10
20 to 24 in.	$1.00	
15 to 20 in.	.75	$6.00

C. Deodara. HIMALAYAN, OR DEODARA CEDAR. The Great Cedar of the Himalayan Mountains. A stately tree, attaining a height of 50 to 75 feet; foliage glaucous green; branches feathery and spreading; perfectly adapted to this climate. We grow this very largely.

	Each	10
30 to 36 in.	$1.50	
24 to 30 in.	1.00	
20 to 24 in.	.75	
15 to 20 in.	.50	$4.00

Cephalotaxus. False Yew.

Cephalotaxus drupacea. This is a very rare and dwarf-growing Yew, which is almost trailing in its habit. Excellent for rocks and ground-covering, or where a low, spreading evergreen is desired. We have an exceptionally fine stock of this most valuable, popular evergreen.

	Each	10	100
18 to 24 in. plants, from 4-in. pots	$0.75		
15 to 18 in. plants, from 3-in. pots	.50	$4.00	$35.00

C. Fortunei. FORTUNE'S YEW. This is a most graceful species, of spreading growth; leaves long, dark green and shining above. Branches long and slender. Attains a height of about 12 to 15 feet.

	Each	10
5 to 6 ft., extra heavy	$3.00	
4 to 5 ft., extra heavy	2.00	$17.50
3 to 4 ft., extra heavy	1.50	12.50
30 to 36 in., very heavy	1.00	8.00
24 to 30 in., heavy	.75	6.00
18 to 24 in.	.50	4.00

C. pedunculata. (*Podocarpus Japonica*). STEM-FRUITED YEW. A medium-sized tree of compact and rather bushy habit; leaves from 1 to 2 inches long, dark, glossy green. A beautiful variety. Ultimate height, 10 to 15 feet.

	Each	10
18 to 24 in., branched, from pots	$1.00	
15 to 18 in., branched, from pots	.75	
12 to 15 in., branched, from pots	.50	$4.00

C. pedunculata fastigiata. (*Podocarpus Koraiana*). KOREAN YEW. An upright-growing variety of bushy habit, with narrow, dark green foliage. Very hardy and desirable. Ultimate height, 6 to 8 feet.

	Each	10
30 to 36 in., well branched	$1.00	$7.50
24 to 30 in., well branched	.75	6.00
18 to 24 in., well branched	.50	4.00

Cunninghamia

Cunninghamia Sinensis. CHINESE PINE. A beautiful tree, resembling somewhat the araucaria. Leaves lance-like on horizontal branches; rapid and symmetrical grower; very scarce. We offer a limited stock of home-grown, thrifty plants.

	Each
10 to 12 in., from pots	$1.00
6 to 8 in., from pots	.50

Cupressus. Cypress.

We grow several varieties of Cupressus which do wonderfully well in this section of the South. Some varieties are particularly adapted to the tropical and sub-tropical sections where they are exceedingly fast growers and make wonderfully fine trees. The majority of the Cupressus in habit of growth are graceful and drooping, and the foliage is feathery; other varieties are of erect and formal growth.

PRICES, unless otherwise noted:

	Each	10	100
4 to 5 ft.	$2.50	$20.00	
3 to 4 ft.	1.50	12.50	$100.00
2 to 3 ft.	1.00	8.00	70.00
18 to 24 inches	.75	6.00	50.00
15 to 18 inches	.50	4.00	30.00

Cupressus Arizonica. ARIZONA CYPRESS. This beautiful conifer is a native of Arizona and New Mexico, and it is found growing at an altitude of from 5,000 to 8,000 feet. It is one of the hardiest of the Cupressus family. This tree attains a height of from 40 to 70 feet, and is of upright, pyramidal habit.

Cephalotaxus drupacea.

55

CUPRESSUS. CYPRESS—Continued.

The foliage is as blue in many instances as Koster's Blue Spruce. This is a very hardy, rare and valuable conifer.

	Each	10
4 to 5 ft.	$2.50	
3 to 4 ft.	2.00	
2 to 3 ft.	1.50	$12.50
18 to 24 inches	1.00	8.00
15 to 18 inches	.75	

C. Benthami. A variety with horizontal branches, forming a dense pyramidal head. Foliage green.

C. Elegans. Feathery foliage of a glaucous tint. A very handsome and graceful variety. Ultimate height, thirty to forty feet.

C. Excelsa. Erect growth. Foliage of ashy hue. Ultimate height 20 to 30 feet.

C. Glauca. Foliage ashy green; rapid and upright grower. Ultimate height, 40 to 50 feet.

C. Glauca pendula. Foliage ashy-green. A rapid grower with pendulous branches; ultimate height, 40 to 50 feet.

C. Goveniana. Of rapid growth and compact habit; foliage bright-green; height, 30 to 40 ft.

C. Gracilis. Ashy green foliage and of a graceful habit. Ultimate height, 30 to 40 feet.

C. Knightiana. Foliage of glaucus hue. Exceedingly graceful; of rapid growth. Ultimate height, 40 to 50 feet.

Cephalotaxus pedunculata fastigiata, Korean Yew.

Cupressus Majestica viridis.
4-ft. plant in nursery, showing typical growth.

C. Macnabiana sulphurea. A new variety; foliage glaucous green with golden tips, an extremely beautiful conifer.

	Each	10
18 to 24 inches	$0.75	$6.00

C. Macrocarpa. MONTEREY CYPRESS. This forms a fine tree fifteen to forty feet in height, with spreading branches and fine, dark-green foliage. In California this variety is extensively planted for hedges and wind breaks.

C. Majestica viridis. A very rare and beautiful form of Majestica. Foliage feathery and of a bright green. Under side of foliage is silvery, and tree is a very compact form. One of the very few conifers which retains its bright green color throughout the entire winter. A most welcome addition to our list of conifers. We offer a limited quantity of strong, grafted plants.

	Each
4 to 5 ft., grafted, very heavy	$3.00
3 to 4 ft., grafted, very heavy	2.00
2 to 3 ft., grafted, heavy	1.00
18 to 24 inches, grafted	.75
15 to 18 inches, grafted	.50

C. sempervirens pyramidalis. ORIENTAL, OR ITALIAN CYPRESS. This well known and popular Conifer is

AUGUSTA, GEORGIA.

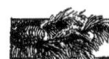

CUPRESSUS. CYPRESS—Continued.

most desirable where a formal effect is desired. It is of compact and shaft-like habit; ultimate height, 60 to 80 feet.

	Each	10
7 to 8 ft., specimens	$4.00	$35.00
6 to 7 ft., specimens	3.00	25.00
5 to 6 ft., specimens	2.00	15.00
4 to 5 ft., specimens	1.25	10.00
3 to 4 ft., strong	1.00	7.50
30 to 36 in., strong	.75	6.00
24 to 30 in., strong	.50	4.00
18 to 24 in., strong	.35	3.00

C. sempervirens Royalii. (*C. Whitleyana*) The most compact and shaft-like of the Cupressus. Forms a main stem from which very small branches radiate. A very distinct and desirable species; grows to a height of 50 to 60 feet.

	Each	10
7 to 8 ft., specimens	$4.00	$35.00
6 to 7 ft., specimens	3.00	25.00
5 to 6 ft., specimens	2.00	15.00
4 to 5 ft., specimens	1.25	10.00

Cupressus Glauca.

	Each	10
3 to 4 ft., strong	$1.00	$7.50
30 to 36 in., strong	.75	6.00
24 to 30 in., strong	.50	4.00
18 to 24 in., strong	.35	3.00

Juniperus. Juniper.

Conifers of easy growth, hardy and long-lived. This splendid group is becoming annually more popular. They are most effective in landscape plantings. The different tones of green are very pleasing when properly planted in groups, using the taller varieties for the back-ground and graduating the plants until the creeping forms are in front; thus forming an exquisite effect.

Juniperus communis. EUROPEAN, OR COMMON JUNIPER. One of the best and hardiest varieties with spreading, erect branches. There are several forms of this Juniper, some of them forming a tree 30 to 40 ft. high.

	Each	10
6 to 7 ft., very heavy, compact specimens	$4.00	
5 to 6 ft., very heavy, compact specimens	3.00	
4 to 5 ft., very heavy, compact specimens	2.00	
3 to 4 ft., very heavy, compact specimens	1.00	
18 to 24 inches, compact specimens	.50	$4.00

J. communis aurea. GOLDEN JUNIPER. A beautiful form of almost trailing habit. Foliage of bright golden hue. Very hardy. A most desirable and effective Juniper.

	Each	10
12 to 18 in., spread, strong	$0.50	$4.00

J. Hibernica. IRISH JUNIPER. A distinct and beautiful variety of erect, dense, columnar shape, resembling a pillar of green. Attains a height of 8 to 10 feet.

	Each	10	100
6 to 7 ft., very heavy	$3.00	$25.00	
5 to 6 ft., very heavy	2.00	15.00	
4 to 5 ft., very heavy	1.50	12.50	$100.00
3 to 4 ft., heavy	.75	6.00	50.00
2 to 3 ft., heavy	.50	4.00	30.00

J. Japonica. (*J. Chinensis*). JAPANESE JUNIPER. One of the most desirable of all the Junipers. It adapts itself to a great range of climate, temperature and soil. A distinct and beautiful variety with bright-green foliage which does not change during winter; of pyramidal and compact growth. Ultimate height, 15 to 20 feet.

	Each	10
3 to 4 ft., very heavy	$2.50	
2 to 3 ft., heavy	1.00	
18 to 24 inches	.75	$6.00
12 to 18 inches	.50	4.00

J. Japonica oreo variegata. VARIEGATED JAPANESE JUNIPER. A beautiful, hardy variety of dwarf habit. Foliage dark-green spotted gold.

	Each	10
24 to 30 in., very bushy	$2.50	
18 to 24 in., very bushy	$1.50	
15 to 18 in., very bushy	1.00	
12 to 15 in., bushy	.50	$4.00

J. oblonga. NEPAUL JUNIPER. Upright habit, with slender, diverging and recurving branches. Can be sheared in different shapes. Ultimate height, 10 to 15 feet.

	Each	10
3½ to 4 ft. by 3-3½ ft, spread, extra heavy, compact specimens	$5.00	
30 to 36 in., by 30 to 36 inch spread, extra heavy specimens	2.50	
18 to 24 inches, compact	1.00	
15 to 18 inches, compact	.50	$4.00

J. Sabina cupressifolia. A procumbent variety of much beauty. Foliage bluish-green; almost creeping in habit.

	Each
15 to 18 in.	$0.75
12 to 15 in.	.50

J. Sabina Tamariscifolia. TAMARIX-LEAVED JUNIPER. A dwarf, almost trailing variety; leaves on the matured part of the branches needle-shaped, of a grayish-green. Very beautiful.

	Each	10
15 to 18 in., heavy	$1.00	$8.00
12 to 15 in., heavy	.75	6.00
10 to 12 in.	.50	4.00

P. J. BERCKMANS CO.

JUNIPERUS. JUNIPER—Continued.

J. Sinensis argentea variegata. VARIEGATED CHINESE JUNIPER. Foliage somewhat similar to J. Japonica, but plant is more compact and dwarf growth; branches beautifully variegated gold and yellow. This is a very hardy and most desirable variety.

	Each	10
3¼ to 4 ft., beautiful, compact specimens	$4.00	$30.00
3 to 3½ ft., compact specimens	3.00	
30 to 36 in., compact specimens	2.00	17.50
24 to 30 in., compact specimens	1.50	12.50
18 to 24 in., compact specimens	1.00	8.00
15 to 18 in., compact	.75	6.00
12 to 15 in., compact	.50	4.00

J. Squamata. A very hardy trailing variety of great merit. Foliage glaucous green. A most valuable plant for rockeries, slopes or where a trailing effect is desired.

	Each	10
3 to 4 ft spread, heavy, well-branched	$3.00	
2 to 3 ft. spread, heavy, well-branched	2.00	
18 to 24 in. spread, well-branched	1.00	$8.00
15 to 18 in. spread, well-branched	.75	6.00
12 to 15 in. spread, well-branched	.50	4.00

J. Suecica. SWEDISH JUNIPER. Foliage light green; very compact. Ultimate height, 10 feet.

	Each	10
3 to 4 ft., very heavy	$1.25	$10.00
2 to 3 ft., very heavy	1.00	8.00
18 to 24 in., heavy	.75	6.00
15 to 18 in., heavy	.50	4.00

J. Virginiana. RED CEDAR. Our native Cedar. Can supply a fine lot of nursery-grown, transplanted plants.

	Each	10
4 to 5 ft., compact	$1.00	
3 to 4 ft., compact	.75	$6.00
2 to 3 ft., compact	.50	4.00

Juniperus sinensis argentea variegata.

J. Virginiana glauca. BLUE VIRGINIA CEDAR. Similar in growth to the common Cedar. Foliage a rich silvery blue, retaining its color well through the entire year. A magnificent variety.

	Each	10
5 to 6 ft., compact specimens	$4.00	
4 to 5 ft., compact specimens	3.00	
3 to 4 ft., compact	1.50	
2 to 3 ft., compact	1.00	
18 to 24 in.	.75	$6.00
15 to 18 in.	.50	4.00

Libocedrus

Libocedrus decurrens. INCENSE CEDAR. A tall, stately tree of compact, upright growth; foliage beautiful, dark-green. A native of the north-western section of America; attains a height of 75 to 100 feet.

	Each	10
18 to 24 in., compact	$1.00	
15 to 18 in., compact	.75	$6.00
12 to 15 in.	.50	4.00

Pinus. Pine.

Pinus densiflora. JAPANESE RED PINE. This is the pine which is dwarfed by the Japanese and trained into many curious and fantastic shapes, but if allowed to grow the tree will attain a height of 75 to 100 feet. A rapid and hardy grower; leaves slender, bright, bluish green, 3 to 5 inches long. A very ornamental variety.

	Each	10
2 to 3 ft.	$0.75	$6.00

P. excelsa. (*Nepalensis*). BHOTAN PINE. Resembles the native White Pine, but leaves much longer and more glaucous, and of more graceful habit; a tree of more compact growth; hardy as far north as Massachusetts, and does remarkably well in the South. In India it is known as the "Drooping Fir."

	Each	10
3 to 4 ft., heavy well-branched	$2.50	
2 to 3 ft., heavy, well-branched	1.25	$10.00
18 to 24 in., heavy, well-branched	1.00	8.00
15 to 18 in., heavy, well-branched	.75	6.00
12 to 15 in., well-branched	.50	4.00

Juniperus oblonga.

AUGUSTA, GEORGIA.

PINUS. PINE—Continued.

P. Koraiensis. KOREAN PINE. This is a beautiful and very hardy Pine of dense and rather dwarf growth; leaves glossy dark green on convex side; bluish-white on flat side. This is a most desirable variety of Pine for this section.

	Each
2 to 3 ft., well-branched	$1.50
18 to 24 in., well-branched	1.00
15 to 18 in.	.50

P. Maritima. (*P. Pinaster*). CLUSTER PINE. Of a pyramidal growth, with spreading branches, slightly pendulous; a rapid grower. Branches reddish-brown; leaves twisted, of a bright, glossy green. Does well near the coast. Ultimate height 60 to 80 feet.

	Each
4 to 5 ft., very heavy, well-branched	$2.50
18 to 24 in., heavy, well-branched	.75
15 to 18 in., well-branched	.50

Retinospora (Chamaecyparis)
Japan Cypress.

Retinospora filifera. THREAD-BRANCHED RETINOSPORA. A beautiful variety, with light green, thread-like foliage, and slender, drooping branches; of medium height. A very hardy and desirable sort.

	Each	10
24 to 30 in., compact	$1.50	$12.50
18 to 24 in., compact	1.00	8.00
15 to 18 in., compact	.75	6.00
12 to 15 in., compact	.50	4.00

R. Filifera aurea. Similar to R. Filifera, but the slender, drooping foliage is golden; of dwarf growth; very desirable where a low effect is wanted.

	Each	10
15 to 18 in., compact	$1.00	$8.00
12 to 15 in., compact	.75	6.00
10 to 12 in., compact	.50	4.00

R. Obtusa. HINOKA CYPRESS. A very fine old variety, vigorous grower with horizontal branches; pendulous foliage, bright, shiny-green with whitish lines beneath.

	Each
3 to 4 feet	$1.50
2 to 3 feet	1.00

Pinus excelsa, Bhotan Pine.

Retinospora filifera. Specimen Plant.

R. Obtusa nana. DWARF JAPANESE CYPRESS. The most dwarf of all the Retinosporas; a very compact grower; foliage very dark-green; very hardy and desirable; seldom attains a height of over 5 feet. This is a favorite variety used by the Japanese for growing in grotesque shapes.

	Each	10	100
2 to 3 ft., compact specimens	$2.00	$15.00	
18 to 24 in., compact	1.50	12.50	
10 to 12 in., compact	.75	6.00	$50.00
8 to 10 in., compact	.50	4.00	35.00

R. Pisifera. PEA-FRUITED CYPRESS. Foliage, bright-green, somewhat pendulous. This is a very valuable and hardy form, and is not commonly grown.

	Each	10
24 to 30 in., compact	$1.50	
18 to 24 in., compact	1.00	$8.00
15 to 18 in., compact	.75	6.00
12 to 15 in., compact	.50	4.00

R. pisifera argentea. SILVER-TIPPED JAPAN CYPRESS. A beautiful variety of very dwarf and compact growth. Ends of branches are silver-tipped. Very desirable.

	Each	10
12 to 15 in., very compact	$1.00	$8.00
10 to 12 in., very compact	.75	6.00
8 to 10 in., very compact	.50	4.00

R. Pisifera aurea. GOLDEN PEA-FRUITED CYPRESS. In foliage and habit of growth similar to R. Pisifera, except that the new growth is of a rich, golden hue; a very showy and valuable variety. Ultimate height 20 to 25 feet.

	Each	10
4 to 5 ft., very compact	$4.00	
3 to 4 ft., very compact	2.50	
2 to 3 ft., very compact	1.25	$10.00
18 to 24 in., compact	.75	6.00
15 to 18 in., compact	.50	4.00

P. J. BERCKMANS CO.

RETINOSPORA—Continued.

R. plumosa. PLUME-LIKE CYPRESS. A rapid-growing variety, with exquisite dark green foliage, the ends of the limbs drooping. Ultimate height, 10 to 15 feet. Ultimate height 20 to 25 feet.

	Each	10
18 to 24 in., compact	$1.00	$8.00
15 to 18 in., compact	.75	6.00
12 to 15 in., compact	.50	4.00

R. Plumosa aurea. GOLDEN PLUMED CYPRESS. This is one of the best, hardiest and most desirable Retinosporas. Vigorous grower. Retains its color constantly; attractive. Ultimate height, 15 to 25 feet.

	Each	10
3 to 4 ft., compact specimens	$3.00	
30 to 36 in., very compact	1.50	$12.50
24 to 30 in., very compact	1.25	
18 to 24 in., very compact	1.00	8.00
15 to 18 in., compact	.75	6.00
12 to 15 in., compact	.50	4.00

R. squarrosa Sieboldi. A rather dwarf but compact grower. Foliage bluish, changing to a purplish hue in winter; an attractive and conspicuous variety.

	Each	10
18 to 24 in., compact	$0.75	$6.00
15 to 18 in., compact	.50	4.00

R. squarrosa Veitchii. VEITCH'S SILVER CYPRESS. Rapid grower; heath-like foliage; bluish-green; handsome and distinct. Ultimate height, 15 to 25 feet.

	Each
24 to 30 in., very compact, sheared	$1.25
18 to 24 in., very compact, sheared	.75
15 to 18 in., very compact, sheared	.50

TAXODIUM. Bald Cypress. (See Deciduous Trees.)

Thuya. Arbor-vitae.

AMERICAN SECTION

Note—All of the Thuyas have an abundance of small fibrous roots, and, therefore, transplant well. All of the plants have been sheared, and are, therefore, compact.

Thuya elegantissima, or lutea. PEABODY'S GOLDEN ARBORVITAE. Of dwarf, compact growth; foliage of bright golden color, which is intensified during winter.

	Each
24 to 30 in., compact	$1.50
18 to 24 in., compact	1.00
15 to 18 in., compact	.75
12 to 15 in.	.50

T. occidentalis. AMERICAN ARBOR-VITAE. A variety which grows naturally from Nova Scotia to the mountains of north Georgia. In this locality it will attain a height of 15 to 25 feet. Of erect form; adapts itself to a wide range of territory and soils. Very popular in the East and West for hedge purposes. Desirable as single specimens.

	Each	10
15 to 18 in., compact	$0.50	$4.00

T. Gigantea. (*T. Lobbii*; *T. plicata*). LOBB'S ARBORVITAE. A tall-growing variety from California. In this section will not attain a height of over 15 to 25 feet; compact grower; foliage glossy green.

	Each	10
18 to 24 in., compact	$0.75	
15 to 18 in., compact	.50	4.00

T. Globosa. GLOBE ARBOR-VITAE. A very dwarf, compact variety of spherical growth; stands shearing well; fine for formal effect, also for vases. Ultimate height 4 to 6 feet.

	Each	10
2 to 2½ ft., very compact	$2.00	
18 to 24 in., very compact	1.50	
15 to 18 in., very compact	1.00	
12 to 15 in., very compact	.75	
10 to 12 in., compact	.50	$4.00

T. Pumila. BOOTH'S ARBOR-VITAE. A very dwarf, compact grower, with bright-green foliage; globe-like form; very desirable where formal effect is desired. Ultimate height 4 to 5 feet.

	Each	10
2 to 2½ ft., very compact	$2.00	
18 to 24 in., very compact	1.50	
15 to 18 in., very compact	1.00	
12 to 15 in., very compact	.75	
10 to 12 in., compact	.50	$4.00

T. Reedii. A somewhat dwarf variety of rather slow growth; of compact, pyramidal habit; a rare and desirable variety; attains an ultimate height of 10 to 15 feet.

	Each	10
15 to 18 in., compact	$0.75	$6.00
12 to 15 in., compact	.50	4.00

All the above Arborvitaes have abundant small roots, and transplant well.

Specimen Conifers

For a number of years we have been growing large quantities of Specimen Conifers. These plants have been very carefully grown. They have been several times transplanted and sheared, and are perfect specimens. To those desiring immediate effect, and who do not mind the cost, we can recommend these Specimen Conifers. Many of the plants offered in the accompanying list are upwards of twenty years of age. The photogsaph shown on page 59 will give an idea of the immediate results obtained by these plants. They are lifted with a large ball of earth about the roots, which is carefully wrapped with moss and burlap. In shipping the plants, they are carefully crated, except in carload lots, when it is not necessary to crate them.

Biota aurea conspicua

	Each
12 to 14 ft. by 4½ ft. in diameter, beautiful, compact specimens	$35.00
11 to 12 ft. by 4 ft. in diameter, beautiful, compact specimens	25.00
10 to 12 ft. by 4 ft. in diameter, beautiful, compact specimens	20.00
9 to 10 ft. by 30 to 36 inches in diameter; beautiful, compact specimens	15.00
8 to 9 ft. by 24 to 30 inches in diameter, beautiful, compact specimens	10.00
7 to 8 ft. by 24 to 30 inches in diameter, beautiful, compact specimens	7.00

Biota aurea pyramidalis

	Each
10 to 12 ft. by 30 to 36 in. diam.	$15.00
8 to 10 ft. by 2½ ft., perfect compact specimens	10.00
7 to 8 ft. by 2 to 2½ ft., perfect, compact specimens	6.00
6 to 7 ft. by 2 ft., perfect, compact specimens	5.00

Cupressus sempervirens pyramidalis

12 to 15 ft., beautiful specimens	$15.00
10 to 12 ft., beautiful specimens	10.00
8 to 10 ft., beautiful specimens	7.50

Juniperus communis Each

10 to 12 ft., beautiful specimens	$10.00
8 to 10 ft., beautiful specimens	7.50
7 to 8 ft., beautiful specimens	5.00

Juniperus Communis Compacta Each

8 to 10 ft., beautiful specimens	$7.50

Juniperus oblonga Each

4 to 5 ft. by 3 ft., compact, sheared specimens	$10.00

Juniperus Sinensis argentea variegata Each 10

3½ to 4 ft., beautiful, compact specimens	$4.00	$30.00

Retinospora plumosa Each

14 ft. by 9 ft.	$50.00
12 ft. by 10 ft.	50.00
12 ft. by 6 ft.	40.00
8 ft. by 6 ft.	20.00
8 ft. by 5 ft.	20.00

Retinospora plumosa aurea Each

10 ft. by 8 ft., beautiful, compact, sheared specimens	$50.00
8 ft. by 8 ft.	35.00
6 ft. by 5 to 6 ft.	20.00
5 ft. by 3 ft.	10.00
3 to 4 ft., very compact specimens	3.00

Retinospora pisifera Each

10 ft. by 9 ft., beautiful, compact, sheared specimens	$50.00
9 ft. by 7 ft.	35.00
7 ft. by 6 ft.	25.00
6 ft. by 5½ ft.	15.00

AUGUSTA, GEORGIA.

SPECIMEN CONIFERS—Continued

Retinospora pisifera argentea

	Each
4 ft. by 5 ft.	$15.00
30 in. by 30 in., perfect, compact specimens	5.00
24 in. by 24 in., perfect, compact specimens	3.00

Retinospora pisifera aurea

	Each
8 ft. by 6 ft.	$20.00
6½ ft. by 5 ft.	20.00
6 ft. by 6 ft.	20.00
6 ft. by 4½ ft.	15.00
5 ft. by 4 ft.	10.00

Thuya Globosa

	Each
30 in. by 30 in., beautiful, compact specimens	$ 4.00

Thuya Reidii

7 ft. by 5 ft.	$15.00
5 to 6 ft., by 4 to 4½ ft.	$10.00

In addition to the above Specimen Conifers, we can supply some beautiful plants of a few other sorts.

Prices and description will be given upon application.

Roses at Fruitland Nurseries.

A Bed of Roses at Fruitlands.

Strong, field-grown roses have always been one of our specialties. This year we have upwards of thirty acres of Roses in our Nurseries.

For many years our Roses have been noted for their sturdiness and unusual vigor. Our soil seems to be especially adapted to the Rose, and our one-year field-grown plants equal the two-year, field-grown plants of the North and West. No garden, no matter how small, is complete without Roses, and no landscape scheme should be made without providing a place for the Rose.

We grow Roses on own roots, and also budded on Manetti stock. Some varieties of Roses do not give satisfactory results unless budded. The budded Roses are especially desirable for Florida and sub-tropical sections, as the roots penetrate the soil to a greater depth than the own-root plants.

All varieties described in this catalogue have been thoroughly tried out in our grounds. We annually test all of the leading new sorts. Many of these new sorts will never appear in our catalogue, as they do not measure up to our standard. Before offering Roses to our customers we must be assured that they are good growers and free bloomers.

DIRECTIONS FOR PLANTING, PRUNING AND FERTILIZING ROSES

Almost any good garden soil, which is well drained is suitable for Roses, but it must be well broken up and put in good condition before planting. It should be well fertilized with decomposed stable manure, bone meal, or a high-grade commercial fertilizer. Be sure that the fertilizer is thoroughly incorporated with the soil. Never plant Roses under large trees or where the ground is taken up by the roots of adjacent trees. If you want to get good Roses, keep the ground free from grass and weeds, and thoroughly cultivated in summer. A mulching in the fall with stable manure or leafmold is beneficial. During the growing season a small amount of bone meal or liquid manure, applied at intervals of a month or six weeks, will give beneficial results.

Before Planting. All Roses need pruning when being transplanted; otherwise the plants will produce inferior blooms. Cut off all but two or three of the strongest branches, and these must be cut back to three to six inches above ground, according to the vigor of the bush. The hole in which the plants are to be set must be of ample size, and after the plants are set, do not fail to water and firm the earth well about the roots.

Pruning. After the first killing frost, or when the Roses are thoroughly matured, two-thirds of the past year's growth should be cut off. As a general rule the more vigorous the variety the less it should be pruned. Remove all decayed wood, and, when pruning, cut off close to the main stems or limbs. Do not leave ragged or jagged stems, as these decay and injure the plant. Climbing Roses should have only their side branches shortened in. Do not disturb the main stem. Ofcourse, all weak and spindling growth should be removed.

We frequently receive complaints from our patrons who order late in the spring. They state that the flowers produced are inferior and do not come up to description. It should be understood that perfect flowers cannot be had when the plants are set out late in February or March, and which produce blooms before they are well established. But if these plants are allowed to grow until the following fall and recive the proper treatment as to pruning, fertilization and cultivation, there will be no cause for complaint.

Note—the letter following each Rose denotes the class to which it belongs, (T.) Tea. (H. T.) Hybrid Tea, (C.) China, (H. P.) Hybrid Perpetual, (N) Noisette, (P.) Polyantha, (R.) Rugosa, (W.) Wichuraiana, (B.) Bourbon.

P. J. BERCKMANS CO.

New and Scarce Roses.

Strong, 1-year, field-grown plants .... Each $0.50 10 $4.00

British Queen. (H. T.) A new English rose. Awarded gold medal at the National Rose Association of England. Before expanding the bud is slightly tinted pink, but pure white when fully developed; free flowering; very fragrant.
Hugo Roller. (T.) Rich, lemon yellow; petals edged and suffused with crimson; free bloomer; vigorous grower.
Jonkeer J. L. Mock. (H. T.) A very strong grower and free bloomer; blooms clear imperial pink; of perfect form and very fragrant. Magnificent bedding variety.
Lady Hillingdon. (T.) Apricot yellow; beautiful bud; strong and vigorous grower; free bloomer.
Lady Pirrie. (H. T.) Buff, tinted salmon. Extremely vigorous grower and free bloomer.
Leslie Holland. (H. T.) Dark scarlet crimson shaded velvety crimson; large flowers; a free and profuse bloomer; highly scented; a superior variety.
Lyon. (H. T.) buds long, tipped coral-red and chrome yellow at base; when buds are fully opened the color is salmon pink shaded chrome in center; very desirable.
Mme. Meleine Soupert. (T.) Center deep yellow, edged and shaded peach pink; bud long; very double.
Mrs. Geo. Shawyer. (T.) This variety is already a great favorite. It is a free bloomer and a vigorous grower. The color is a bright pink; long pointed buds; stems very long.
President Taft. (T.) A beautiful shade of deep, shining pink; blooms very large and of fine form; very fragrant. This Rose is in a class by itself.
Senateur Mascarand. (H. T.) Deep orange-yellow, lighter at edge of petals; flowers large and full; a good grower and a free bloomer.
Robin Hood. (H. T.) Flowers large, full, very double; rosy scarlet; fine foliage; free bloomer and a vigorous grower.
Sunburst. (T.) This beautiful Rose has been tested for three years, and it easily stands at the head of all sorts of its color. The color is a most pleasing shade of yellow and orange; buds long and pointed; plant vigorous and healthy; blooms keep for a long time after being cut. A grand Rose.

Note—In addition to the above new roses we can supply a few plants each of other desirable new varieties Some of the roses above enumerated can only be supplied budded on Manetti Stock. The prices as quoted apply to plants on own roots or budded.

Roses on Their Own Roots.

PRICES, except where noted:
                                                        Each   10   100
Purchaser's selection, strong,
 one-year, field-grown plants $0.25 $2.50 $20.00
Our selection, in 25 or 50 varieties,
 strong, one-year, field-
 grown plants 2.00   17.50
Can supply a limited number of
 strong, two-year, field-grown
 Roses of nearly all of the varieties
 listed below 50   3.50   30.00

Anna de Diesbach. (H. P.) Clear, bright carmine pink; very large, full and finely shaped; fragrant and a free bloomer.
Antoine Rivoire. (T.) Yellow, tinted rosy flesh, with a border of carmine. Good form. A fine rose.
Blumenschmidt. (H. T.) Pure citron yellow; outer petals edged tender rose; vigorous grower; fine variety.
Catherine Zeimet. (P.) (*Double White Baby Rambler*). This is a very profuse and perpetual bloomer; the buds are pure white, about one to one and one-fourth inches in diameter; plant grows to a height of about twenty inches; compact habit; excellent for a dwarf hedge. $15.00 per 100.
Clio. (H. P.) Flesh, shaded with rosy-pink; large bud; of fine form.
Clothilde Soupert. (P.) Flowers 1½ inches in diameter, beautifully formed; white, with rose or light carmine center; a constant bloomer; a desirable variety for cemeteries.
Col. R. S. Williamson. (T.) Satiny-white with deep flesh center; flowers very full, of perfect form, with high pointed center. A fine rose.
Countess of Gosford. (H. T.) Salmon shaded pink and rose, base of petals saffron yellow. A beautiful Irish variety.
Dean Hole. (H. T.) Deep salmon-pink; buds very long; a very fine, vigorous and free-blooming variety.
Duchesse de Brabant. (*Comtesse de Labarthe*). (T.) Pink shaded to carmine; a favorite and a hardy old variety.
Earl of Dufferin. (H. P.) Very large; crimson shaded maroon.
Etoile de France. (T.) A very vigorous grower. Flowers very large, full, cupped; dark, velvety crimson center vivid cerise. A fine new variety.
Etoile de Lyon. (T.) Golden yellow; very double, vigorous; a free bloomer; very fragrant.
F. R. Patzer. (H. T.) Beautiful and free-blooming; robust, of erect growth; profuse bloomer; flowers creamy-buff, back of petals pink, as the bud opens it changes to light-pink; very fragrant.
Freiherr Von Marschall. (T.) A double form of Papa Gontier. Flowers large and full; color dark carmine-red; buds long; a very free and vigorous grower; foliage very beautiful and distinct.
Gen. McArthur. (H. T.) Dark, velvety scarlet; large; free bloomer; fragrant.
Gloire Lyonnaise. (H. P.) Flowers very large, full; white, with base of petals very light canary-yellow; vigorous grower.
Gruss an Teplitz. (H. T.) Bright crimson; very full; free bloomer. Very good.
Helen Gould. (*Balduin*). (H. T.) Rosy pink; long, pointed buds. Fine.
John Hopper. (H. P.) Bright rose, with carmine center; cupped; well formed.
Kaiserin Augusta Victoria. (H. T.) Creamy white; very double; buds large and pointed. Best white Hybrid Tea grown.
Maman Cochet. (T.) Deep rose-pink; inner side of petals silvery rose; very double. Extra strong grower; fine bloomer. The finest Rose by far that has been introduced for a long time. We can confidently recommend it.
Margaret Dickson. (H. P.) A fine Rose; vigorous grower; flowers white, tinted pink near center.
Marie Pavie. (P.) Pale rose, changing to white; most valuable for low hedges; a most profuse blooming polyantha; blooms continuous from early spring until frost. $15.00 per 100.
Marie Van Houtte. (T.) Pale yellow, edged rose. Very fine.
Meteor. (H. T.) Dark, velvety crimson. Vigorous grower and profuse bloomer.
Mme. Francisca Kruger. (T.) Large, double, coppery-yellow shading to peach; of strong and vigorous growth.
Mme. Helene Gambier. (H. T.) Rosy-salmon with deeper shading; very double and full; an excellent variety.
Mme. Jules Grolez. (H. T.) Satiny-rose color; flowers large, very double; a profuse and free bloomer.
Mme. Lambard. (T.) Bright red; large, full and fragrant.
Mme. Plantier. (H. N.) Bears thousands of pure white, medium-sized flowers. Profuse bloomer in early spring only. Desirable for massing, and as hardy as an oak. $15.00 per 100.
Mrs. Aaron Ward. (H. T.) When in bud the color is coppery orange, changing to orange when partly developed; when fully open is of a pinkish form.
Orleans. (P.) Deep cerise with a distinct white center. A showy and dainty variety of the dwarf Polyantha; superior to Baby Rambler; blooms from early spring until frost; flowers produced in large heads; very dwarf grower; makes an excellent hedge. This, when combined with Catherine Zeimet. in the background, makes a very pleasing effect. $15.00 per 100.
Papa Gontier. (T.) Brilliant carmine, tinted rose; finely formed buds.
Prince Camille de Rohan. (H. P.) Deep, rich, velvety crimson, passing to intense maroon, shading to black. At a short distance the flowers appear really black. One of the handsomest roses, and is worthy of a place in every garden.

ROSES—Continued.

Paul Neyron. (H. P.) The flowers are immense; probably the largest Rose. Bright, shining pink, clear and beautiful; double and full; finely scented; blooms all summer.

Rhea Reid. (H. T.) One of the best Roses of recent introduction. A cross of American Beauty with a red seedling. A vigorous and rapid grower. As large as American Beauty; very double and fragrant; continuous bloomer. Beautiful shade of red.

Rugosa rubra. (R.) A popular variety for planting in masses or for hedges. Large single crimson flowers, followed by glossy red berries.

Souv. de La Malmaison. (B.) Large, very full; flesh colored. A very free bloomer; an old favorite.

Wellesley. (T.) Beautiful pink; the reverse side of the petals silvery.

White Maman Cochet. (T.) Pure white, sometimes tinged blush. A superb Rose.

Wm. Shean. (H. T.) Strong grower, throwing up long, stiff canes, crowned with large, pointed flowers of a Killarney-pink. Fine form; free and perpetual bloomer. A grand Rose.

Wm. R. Smith. (H. T.) A variety combining the good qualities of K. A. Victoria and Maman Cochet. A very free blooming and upright and vigorous grower; flowers creamy-white with shadings of pink.

Zelia Pradel. (T.) White with yellow center; double; free bloomer; half climber, almost evergreen; a very popular old variety.

Climbing Roses on Own Roots

PRICES, except where noted:

	Each	10	100
Purchaser's selection, strong, one-year, field-grown plants.	$0.25	$2.50	$20.00
Our selection, strong, one-year field-grown plants		2.00	17.50
Can supply a limited number of strong, two-year, field-grown Roses of nearly all of the varieties listed above	.50	3.50	30.00

Cherokee. (*Rosa laevigata*). The well-known Cherokee of the South, where it has become naturalized; it is, however, a native of China. A vigorous and rampant climber. Large, single white, fragrant flowers produced in early spring in great profusion; evergreen; foliage bright, glossy green; most desirable for pergolas and trellises. Will climb to the top of the loftiest tree.

Clothilde Soupert, Climbing. (P.) This variety originated in our nurseries. We have cultivated it for years and can recommend it with the utmost confidence. In color and form it is similar to its parent, the well-known Clothilde Soupert, but flowers are larger. A constant bloomer after the first year, as it flowers best on old wood. Vigorous grower, and has resisted a cold of 20 degrees below zero. This is a great addition to our list of Climbing Roses, and is becoming one of the favorites.

Dorothy Perkins. (H. W.) This grand rose is a Hybrid Wichuriana. It is a vigorous and rampant climber. The foliage is of a deep green, leathery texture, and remains on the plant nearly all winter. The flowers are from 1 to 1½ inches in diameter, borne in clusters of from 10 to 30, and very double, of a beautiful shell-pink. Remains in bloom for several weeks. A most desirable Climbing Rose. Most effective for planting on terraces and slopes.

	10	100
Strong, 1 year, field-grown	$0.25 $2.00	$12.50
Strong, 2 year, field-grown	.35 2.50	15.00

Evergreen, or Double Cherokee. This is a double form of the popular Cherokee Rose. The flowers are 2½ to 3 inches in diameter; very double, similar to the White Banksia. The plant being evergreen makes it a desirable climber. Blooms in late spring.

Fortunes' Yellow, or Beauty of Glazenwood. (Climbing). Yellow, flaked with carmine; very good grower; spring bloomer.

Gainsborough. Rosy-flesh; flowers large; a fine variety.

Lady Gay. A bright rose-pink; similar to Dorothy Perkins, but later, the flowers being larger and fewer to the cluster.

Philadelphia Rambler. This variety is a cross between Crimson Rambler and the Hybrid Perpetual, Victor Hugo. Its color is deeper and brighter crimson, flowers larger and growth more erect than Crimson Rambler.

White Banksia. The flowers of this very desirable Rose are pure white, violet-scented, very small, double, and borne in umbels of twelve to fifteen blossoms. Spring bloomer.

Wichuraiana. (The Memorial Rose). Almost evergreen; flowers small, single, white; of trailing habit. Beautiful for planting on slopes and terraces, which it soon covers with a mass of bright green foliage. On account of its hardiness and glossy foliage, it is used extensively in the North for cemetery planting. The plant is a strong grower.

	Each	10	100
Strong, field-grown	$0.25	$2.00	$12.50
Extra strong, 2-year, field-grown	.35	2.50	15.00

Yellow Banksia. Identical with White Banksia in all particulars except the color, which is a clear, sulphur yellow; spring bloomer.

Roses Budded Upon Manetti Stock.

One-year plants, budded low, 35 cents each; $3.00 for 10; $25.00 per 100. We can supply strong, extra heavy, two-year plants, of most of the folowing varieties, at 50 cents each, $3.50 for 10, $30.00 per 100.

It is almost impossible to propagate some varieties of Roses upon their own roots, and unless these are grown upon Manetti, their cultivation would have to be discontinued. Others produce finer flowers when budded or grafted upon the Manetti stock. They are especially desirable for Florida and sub-tropical sections, as their roots penetrate the soil to a great depth, and the plants are thus enabled to withstand extreme heat and drought and still produce flowers.

The photo of a budded rose shows the budded portion, "A" and suckers from the Manetti stock "B." Note the difference in the foliage. That of the Manetti is composed of from seven to nine leaflets; whereas, the tea, hybrid tea, hybrid perpetual and Bourbon roses usually have but five leaflets.

Budded Rose. A. budded part; B. Manetti Stock.

P. J. BERCKMANS CO.

Cherokee Rose.

American Beauty. (H. P.) Deep rose; large; cupped; fragrant; dwarf grower.
Anna de Diesbach. (H. P.) Clear, bright carmine-pink; very large, full and finely shaped; fragrant and a free bloomer.
Baroness de Rothschild. (H. P.) Flowers of large size; color light-pink, beautifully cupped, remarkably symmetrical; a most distinct and beautiful rose; good bloomer; flowers are borne on stout, erect stems.
Captain Christy. (H. T.) Blush, rosy center; large and full; very free bloomer.
Dr. Sewell. (H. P.) Bright crimson, tinged with purple; large, full
Etoile de France. (T.) A very vigorous grower. Flowers very large; full; cupped; dark, velvet crimson; center vivid cerise. A fine variety of recent introduction.
Etoile de Lyon. (T.) Rich golden yellow; vigorous; free bloomer.
Eugene Furst. (H. P.) Strong, vigorous grower, with thick, healthy foliage. Flowers beautiful velvety crimson, shading to maroon. Highly scented.
Frau Karl Druschki. (H. P.) This is deservedly one of the most popular roses grown; flowers pure white; perfect in form; very free bloomer, strong grower, perfectly hardy everywhere. By some is called the White American Beauty; a truly magnificent rose.
Glory of Brussels. Flowers very large; full; of fine form; color deep, velvety amaranth purple, almost black, fiery red at base of petals; one of the best dark roses; very fragrant; free bloomer and vigorous.
Gl. Lyonnaise. (H. P.) Flowers very large, full; white, with base of petals very light canary yellow; vigorous grower.
Grand Mogul. (H. P.) Purplish crimson; large and well formed. A magnificent variety.
Jules Margottin. Fine carmine; flowers large and full, somewhat flat.
Kaiserin Augusta Victoria. (H. T.) Creamy white; very double; buds large and pointed. Decidedly the best white Hybrid Tea grown.
Killarney. A favorite rose, of brilliant silvery-pink; beautiful in bud; flowers large; free bloomer and strong grower.
La France. (H. T.) One of the best known Roses. Silvery peach; excellent; weak grower.
Louis Van Houtte. (H. P.) Vivid, velvety crimson; large, full and fine form. A very fine variety.
Meteor. (T.) Dark, velvety crimson. Vigorous grower and profuse bloomer.
Mlle. Helene Gambier. (H. T.) Rosy salmon, shading deeper; very double and full. Fine variety.
Mme. Caroline Testout. (H. T.) One of the best of the newer Roses. Of La France type, but clear pink; large; free bloomer. A great favorite where known.
Perle des Jardins. (T.) Bright, golden-yellow; flowers large; full; double; very fragrant; a vigorous climber; best of its color.
Prince Camille de Rohan. (H. P.) Deep, rich, velvety crimson, passing to intense maroon, shading to black. At a short distance the flowers appear really black. One of the handsomest roses, and is worthy of a place in every garden.

CLIMBING ROSES BUDDED ON MANETTI.

One-year plants, budded low, 35 cents each; $3.00 for 10; $25.00 per 100. We can supply two-year extra heavy plants of most of the following varieties at 50 cents each; $3.50 for 10; $30.00 per 100

Captain Christy. (H. T.) Blush, rosy center; large and full; very free bloomer.
Devoniensis, Climbing (T.) An old favorite; creamy-white, flesh center; very fragrant; spring bloomer.
Kaiserin Augusta Victoria. Climbing. (*Mrs. Robert Peary*). (T.) Similar to the bush form. White; vigorous.
Lamarque. (N.) Pure white. A favorite old Climbing Rose.
Marechal Niel. (T.) Deep chrome-yellow. Always deeper in color and a better grower when budded.
Meteor, Climbing. (H. T.) Dark, velvety crimson. Vigorous grower and profuse bloomer.
Mme. Caroline Testout. A magnificent free blooming rose with flowers of satiny-pink; large and full; a beautiful climber.
Perle des Jardins. (T.) Bright yellow, very full and double. Best of its color.
Pillar of Gold. (T.) Rosy pink, base of petals yellow. Variable in color. Sometimes almost solid pink.
Pink Cherokee. This superb Rose is a pink form of the well-known Cherokee Rose. It is one of the earliest to bloom. Immense, beautiful, single pink flowers are produced in profusion. The plant blooms for a period of about two months. It is a vigorous and rampant grower; foliage is evergreen and of a bright, glossy green. This is a great acquisition to our list of Roses. Immensely popular.
Reine Marie Henriette. (T.) Bright cherry-red. Of good form and vigorous habit. The best red climber.
Reve d'Or (*Climbing Safrano*). (T.) Chamois-yellow large, full; fragrant; free bloomer. Extra fine.
Solfatarre. (N.) Light yellow; free bloomer.
Souv de La Malmaison. (B.) A beautiful climbing form of this well-known rose; flowers flesh colored, large and very full; rampant grower; evergreen. This variety is becoming a great favorite.
Waltham No. 3. (H. P.) Very fine spring and autumn blooming climber; dark crimson.
William Allen Richardson. (T.) Orange-yellow; center coppery-yellow.
Wootton. (H. P.) Bright magenta-red, richly shaded crimson. very double and fine climber.

Pink Cherokee and Double Cherokee.

Home Floriculture. By Eben E. Rexford. A practical guide to the treatment of flowering and other ornamental plants in the house and garden, intended exclusively for amateur floriculturists, by one of the most successful amateur floriculturists in America. Price $1.00. (O. J. CO.)
The Garden in the Wilderness. By Hanna Rion. A fascinating story of a country home and its garden in the making. Illustrated. Price $1.66. (M. N. CO.)

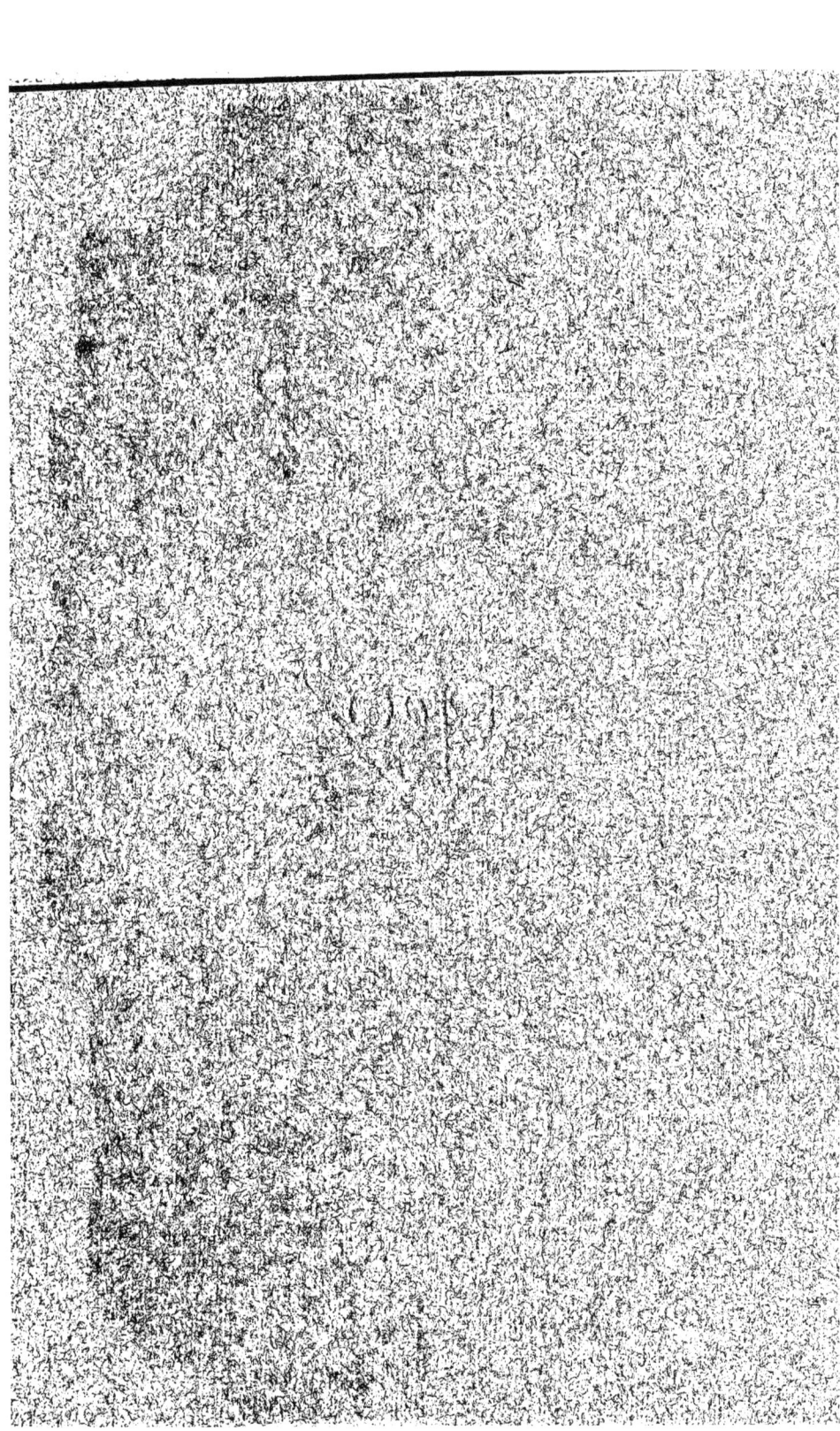

USE

SPRAYING MATERIALS

Manufactured by
Thomsen Chemical Co.
BALTIMORE, MD.

Sold by **BERCKMANS BROS.** Augusta, Ga.

Save Your Fruits and Vegetables and Preserve the Beauty of Your Ornamental Trees and Plants

In recent years insects and fungous diseases have become so numerous and so destructive that it is no longer possible to successfully conduct horticultural operations without spraying. If the proper materials are used and the work is correctly done, fruit trees, vegetables and ornamental plants may be protected from the attacks of these pests, so that their fruitfulness and beauty will not be destroyed.

KIND OF MATERIAL TO USE.

One of the most important considerations in the treatment of your plants is the kind of spray materials to use. Call for "Orchard Brand," and your problem will be solved. Under this brand you will find arsenical poisons for various chewing insects, sulphur and oil solutions for sucking insects and copper and sulphur preparations for fungous diseases. Here they are:

B. T. S. (A dry substitute for lime-sulphur solution); Lime-Sulphur Solution; Atomic Sulphur (A fungicide specially for use on peaches); Bordeaux Mixture; Arsenate of Lead, Standard, Paste or Powder; Arsenite of Zinc, Paste or Powder; Arsenate of Lead, Tri-Plumbic; Bordeaux-Arsenate of Lead Mixture.

BUREAU OF INFORMATION.

We maintain a Research and Special Service Department, which in effect is a free bureau of information for the benefit of our customers. Write us your troubles, and we will prescribe the remedies free of charge. This service covers matters of spraying, pruning, cultivating, fertilizing and other related subjects, and those who take advantage of it obtain the most up-to-date information available.

DIRECTIONS FOR DORMANT SPRAYING.

As a scale remedy on all deciduous fruit trees. use B. T. S. at the rate of 16 pounds to 50 gallons of cold water, or, if preferred, lime-sulphur solution at the rate of 1 gallon to 8 gallons of cold water.

DIRECTIONS FOR PREPARING.

B. T. S.—This material may be dissolved in a bucket and poured into the spray tank, where small quantities are to be used. In large spraying operations the tank may be partially filled with water after which the agitator should be started and the material poured slowly into the spray tank. The agitator should be run continuously while the tank is being filled and a few minutes thereafter in order to insure the dissolving and thorough mixing of all the material.

Lime-Sulphur Solution.—This material is prepared for spraying by simply adding water at the rate of 8 gallons to 1 gallon of the solution, thoroughly stirring the diluted material before the spraying operation commences.

GROWING PERIOD SPRAYING FOR PEACHES.

For the control of curculio, scab and brown rot spray the trees as follows:

(1) About ten days after the petals fall use 1½ pounds or 2 pounds of T. P. arsenate of lead paste, or ¾ pound to 1 pound of powder, and add 3 pounds of lime to each 50 gallons of water;

(2) About three weeks later, or one month after the petals fall, spray the trees with atomic sulphur, 5 pounds to 50 gallons of water, adding to each batch 1½ pounds of T. P. arsenate of lead paste or ¾ pound of powder, and adding 3 pounds of lime to each 50 gallon batch;

(3) About one month before the fruit ripens spray the trees with atomic sulphur, 5 pounds to 50 gallons of water. Poison should not be added at this time.

GROWING PERIOD SPRAYING FOR APPLES.

For the control of the codling moth, curculio, scab and leaf-spot, use 2 pounds of standard arsenate of lead and 3 pounds of B. T. S. to each 50 gallons of water. (1½ gallons of lime-sulphur solution may be substituted for the B. T. S. if preferred).

Spray the trees as follows:

(1) When the cluster buds open, just before blooming; (2) as soon as the petals fall and before the calyx lobes close; (3) three weeks later, (4) about ten weeks after the petals fall.

GROWING PERIOD SPRAYING FOR POTATOES, TOMATOES, ASPARAGUS AND TOBACCO.

For the control of potato beetle, asparagus beetle and tobacco worm, use powdered arsenite of zinc at the rate of 2 pounds of the powder to 50 gallons of water per acre of plants treated. The first application should be made as soon as the insects appear and subsequent applications as required.

For the control of blight and other fungous diseases on potatoes and tomatoes Bordeaux mixture should be used at the rate of 8 pounds to 50 gallons of water. This can be combined with the arsenite.

Note.—For several years we have used "Orchard Brand" Spray Materials exclusively in our own orchards with excellent results, and can supply them to all growers. Prices on insecticides change from time to time. We will always be prepared to quote the lowest market prices, and solicit your inquiries and orders, which should be mailed direct to

BERCKMANS BROTHERS,
AUGUSTA, GA.